First World War
and Army of Occupation
War Diary
France, Belgium and Germany

3 DIVISION
Divisional Troops
Durham Light Infantry
1/9th Battalion Pioneers
1 January 1917 - 31 December 1917

WO95/1405/3

The Naval & Military Press Ltd
www.nmarchive.com
Published in association with The National Archives

Published by

The Naval & Military Press Ltd

Unit 10 Ridgewood Industrial Park,

Uckfield, East Sussex,

TN22 5QE England

Tel: +44 (0) 1825 749494

www.naval-military-press.com

www.nmarchive.com

This diary has been reprinted in facsimile from the original. Any imperfections are inevitably reproduced and the quality may fall short of modern type and cartographic standards.

© **Crown Copyright**
Images reproduced by permission of The National Archives, London, England, 2015.

Contents

Document type	Place/Title	Date From	Date To
Heading	WO95/1405/3		
Heading	BEF 3 Division Northern Div Troops 1/9 Dur. L.I. 1919 Mar To 1919 Oct		
War Diary	Cologne	01/03/1919	31/10/1919
Heading	3rd Division Divl. Troops 20th Battalion K.R.R.C. 1918 Jan-1918 Dec		
War Diary	Mory	01/01/1918	27/01/1918
War Diary	Henin	28/01/1918	28/02/1918
Heading	3rd Divisional Troops 20th Battalion K.R.R.C. (Pioneers) March 1918		
War Diary	Henin	01/03/1918	21/03/1918
War Diary	Niejville Vitaue	22/03/1918	22/03/1918
War Diary	Wailly	23/03/1918	23/03/1918
War Diary	Bellacourt	24/03/1918	29/03/1918
War Diary	Sus. St. Ledger	30/03/1918	31/03/1918
Heading	3rd Division Pioneers War Diary 20th Battalion Kings Royal Rifle Corps (Pioneers) April 1918		
War Diary	Bruay	01/04/1918	03/04/1918
War Diary	Les Brebey	04/04/1918	10/04/1918
War Diary	Labourse	11/04/1918	11/04/1918
War Diary	Gonnehem	12/04/1918	13/04/1918
War Diary	Choques	14/04/1918	30/04/1918
War Diary	Chocques	01/05/1918	31/05/1918
Miscellaneous	20th (S) Battalion Kings Royal Rifle Corps (Pioneers)		
Miscellaneous	Addendum No.1 To D.104 Action In Case Of Attack		
Miscellaneous	20th (S) Battalion Kings Royal Rifle Corps (Pioneers)		
War Diary	Chocques	01/06/1918	01/06/1918
War Diary	Mareowet	02/06/1918	28/06/1918
War Diary	Chocques	29/06/1918	29/06/1918
War Diary	Mareowet	29/06/1918	30/06/1918
Miscellaneous	Operation Order No.2	13/06/1918	13/06/1918
War Diary	Chocques Marequet	01/07/1918	06/08/1918
War Diary	Burbure	07/08/1918	08/08/1918
War Diary	Pressey Les Pernes	09/08/1918	12/08/1918
War Diary	Grouches	13/08/1918	19/08/1918
War Diary	Bienvillers	20/08/1918	20/08/1918
War Diary	Purple Reserve	21/08/1918	24/08/1918
War Diary	Purple Line	25/08/1918	27/08/1918
War Diary	Moyenneville	28/08/1918	01/09/1918
War Diary	St Leger (Bank Trench)	01/09/1918	06/09/1918
War Diary	Bienvillers	07/09/1918	09/09/1918
War Diary	Courcelles	10/09/1918	10/09/1918
War Diary	Bucquoy Sheet I 23a 7.7	11/09/1918	23/09/1918
War Diary	I.23a 7.7	24/09/1918	24/09/1918
War Diary	Hermes	25/09/1918	29/09/1918
War Diary	Flesquieres	30/09/1918	30/09/1918
War Diary	Ribecourt	01/10/1918	12/10/1918
War Diary	Crevecoeur	13/10/1918	19/10/1918
War Diary	Quievy	21/10/1918	23/10/1918
War Diary	Solesmes	24/10/1918	05/11/1918

War Diary	Ruesnes	06/11/1918	12/11/1918
War Diary	Gommegnies	15/11/1918	15/11/1918
War Diary	Neufmesnil	16/11/1918	16/11/1918
War Diary	Louvroil	18/11/1918	18/11/1918
War Diary	Cousolre	20/11/1918	22/11/1918
War Diary	Thuin	23/11/1918	23/11/1918
War Diary	Nalinnes	24/11/1918	24/11/1918
War Diary	Biesmes	25/11/1918	25/11/1918
War Diary	Rouillon	26/11/1918	26/11/1918
War Diary	Najoye	27/11/1918	29/11/1918
War Diary	Pessoux	30/11/1918	31/11/1918
Heading	On His Majesty's Service. 20th K.R.R.C (Pioneers) December 1918		
War Diary	Pessoux	01/12/1918	03/12/1918
War Diary	Baillon Ville	04/12/1918	04/12/1918
War Diary	Melreux	05/12/1918	05/12/1918
War Diary	Mormont	06/12/1918	06/12/1918
War Diary	Malempre	07/12/1918	07/12/1918
War Diary	Sart	08/12/1918	08/12/1918
War Diary	Bovigny	09/12/1918	10/12/1918
War Diary	Thommen (Germany)	11/12/1918	11/12/1918
War Diary	Heuem	12/12/1918	12/12/1918
War Diary	Hallschlag	13/12/1918	13/12/1918
War Diary	Schmidtheim	14/12/1918	14/12/1918
War Diary	Schonau	15/12/1918	15/12/1918
War Diary	Kirspenich	16/12/1918	16/12/1918
War Diary	Euskirchen	17/12/1918	17/12/1918
War Diary	Fussenich	18/12/1918	18/12/1918
War Diary	Duren	19/12/1918	31/12/1918
War Diary	?	05/12/1918	05/12/1918
War Diary	Mormont	06/12/1918	06/12/1918
War Diary	Empre	07/12/1918	07/12/1918
War Diary	QRT	08/12/1918	08/12/1918
War Diary	Bovigny	09/12/1918	10/12/1918
War Diary	?	11/12/1918	11/12/1918
War Diary	UEM	12/12/1918	12/12/1918
War Diary	Schlag	13/12/1918	13/12/1918
War Diary	Schmidtheim	14/12/1918	14/12/1918
War Diary	Schonau	15/12/1918	15/12/1918
War Diary	Fussenich	16/12/1918	16/12/1918
War Diary	Euskirchen	17/12/1918	17/12/1918
War Diary	Fussenich	18/12/1918	18/12/1918
War Diary	Duren	19/12/1918	31/12/1918
Heading	3rd Division Divl. Troops 20th (S) Battalion K.R.R.C. (Pioneers) Jan-Dec 1917		
Heading	20th (S) Battn. Kings Royal Rifle Corps (Pioneers) War Diary For January 1st 1917 To January 31st 1917 Volume X		
War Diary	Courcelles	01/01/1917	07/01/1917
War Diary	Montrelet	08/01/1917	08/01/1917
War Diary	Candas	09/01/1917	27/01/1917
War Diary	Sarton	28/01/1917	28/01/1917
War Diary	Houte Visce	29/01/1917	29/01/1917
War Diary	Ceuf	30/01/1917	30/01/1917
War Diary	Bailleul And Corncelles	31/01/1917	31/01/1917
Miscellaneous	O.C. 20th KRRC		

War Diary	Ambrines	01/02/1917	02/02/1917
War Diary	Arras	03/02/1917	28/02/1917
Miscellaneous	O.C. 20th K.R.R.C.		
War Diary	Arras	01/03/1917	31/03/1917
Miscellaneous	From O.C. 20th KRRC To "Q" 3rd Division		
War Diary	Arras	01/04/1917	23/04/1917
War Diary	Filloy	24/04/1917	30/04/1917
Heading	20th (S) Battn. King's Royal Rifle Corps (Pioneers) War Diary Volume XI From 1st May 1917 To 31st May 1917		
War Diary	Filloy	01/05/1917	14/05/1917
War Diary	Agnes-Les-Duissans	15/05/1917	15/05/1917
War Diary	Arras	16/05/1917	21/05/1917
War Diary	Lincourt	22/05/1917	31/05/1917
Miscellaneous	From O.C. 20th KRRC "Q" 3rd Division	30/06/1917	30/06/1917
War Diary	Lincourt	01/06/1917	01/06/1917
War Diary	Filloy	02/06/1917	19/06/1917
War Diary	Lattre St Quentin	20/06/1917	20/06/1917
War Diary	Denier	21/06/1917	27/06/1917
War Diary	Grouches	28/06/1917	30/06/1917
Miscellaneous	From O.C. 20th KRRC To 3rd Division Q	31/07/1917	31/07/1917
Heading	War Diary 20th Kings Royal Rifles (Pioneer) 1st To 31st July 1917		
War Diary	Achiet-Le-Petit	01/07/1917	02/07/1917
War Diary	Nr Haplincourt	03/07/1917	08/07/1917
War Diary	Lebucquiere	09/07/1917	31/07/1917
Heading	Vol 14 20th (S) Bn K.R.R.C. (Pioneers) War Diary-August 1917		
War Diary	3rd Division Q Herewith War Diary For August 1917		
War Diary	Labucquiere	01/08/1917	31/08/1917
Miscellaneous	From O.C. 20th K.R.R.C. (Pioneers) To 3rd Division Q		
War Diary	Labucquiere	01/09/1917	04/09/1917
War Diary	Bertincourt	05/09/1917	15/09/1917
War Diary	Acheit Le Petit	16/09/1917	18/09/1917
War Diary	Watou	19/09/1917	21/09/1917
War Diary	Ypres	22/09/1917	30/09/1917
Miscellaneous	From O.C. 20th Kings Royal Refle		
War Diary	Brandhoek	01/10/1917	04/10/1917
War Diary	Buysscheure	05/10/1917	08/10/1917
War Diary	Elverdinghe	09/10/1917	09/10/1917
War Diary	Canal Bank C25 Central	10/10/1917	27/10/1917
War Diary	Dawsonscorner B.22 d Central	28/10/1917	31/10/1917
Miscellaneous	3rd Division A/3072		
Miscellaneous	20th Kings Royal Rifles		
War Diary	Dawsonscorner B.22.d. Central	01/11/1917	04/11/1917
War Diary	Houtkerque	05/11/1917	05/11/1917
War Diary	Caudescure	06/11/1917	06/11/1917
War Diary	Conneham	07/11/1917	07/11/1917
War Diary	Hersin	08/11/1917	08/11/1917
War Diary	Arras	09/11/1917	09/11/1917
War Diary	Beugnatre	10/11/1917	30/11/1917
Miscellaneous	Appendix A		
War Diary	Beugnatre B30c 4.2	01/12/1917	13/12/1917
War Diary	Mory	15/12/1917	31/12/1917

WO 95
SB 00N
14 05 13

BEF 3 DIVISION

NORTHERN DIV TROOPS

1/9 DUR. L. I.

1919 MAR to 1919 OCT

ORIGINAL CONFIDENTIAL Army Form C. 2118.

WAR DIARY 9th Bn THE DURHAM L.I. INFANTRY
or
INTELLIGENCE SUPPLY. VOLUME XXVIII Page 1

(Erase heading not required.)

Place	Date	Hour	Summary of Events and Information	Remarks and references to Appendices
BOLOGNE	March 1		Billets – baths. Cont.	Apt 4.5
	2		No work. Cont.	
	3		Training. Major T.B Jackson M.C returned from course & took command. Cont.	
	4		Training. Cont.	
	5		Training. Cont.	
	6		G.O.C. 2nd Division inspected the Bn at 10.00 hrs & has C by which sent on detachment guard duty at Königsdorf. Bn won Divi. Rugby Div. football tournament. Cont.	
	7		Baths & short training. Cont.	
	8		Change service Lt Col Horack where from leave. Cont.	
	9		No 325119 Sgt E Dobson. Cont. MILITARY MEDAL AWARDS Cont.	
	10		Cleaning of all equipment. Cont.	
	11		A Coy took on Corps football final. B Coy on their new fullish Bn beaten 2 goals to 1 by 146 RHA in 61 Div tournament Cont	
	12		Route continued. Cont.	
	13		Training. Cont.	

ORIGINAL CONFIDENTIAL

Army Form C. 2118.

WAR DIARY
or
INTELLIGENCE SUMMARY.

9th Bn THE DURHAM LIGHT INFANTRY

VOLUME XLVIII   Page 2

(Erase heading not required.)

Place	Date	Hour	Summary of Events and Information	Remarks and references to Appendices
SOLOGNE	14th		40 men sent to firing party to R.A.F. Draft of 10 Officers & 276 OR received from 15th D.L.I. HONOURS AWARDS. LEGION D'HONNEUR - CROIX DE CHEVALIER Lt Colonel F.G. Crouch DSO. SCM Sr Polonal Bt Polonal.	
	15th		Cleaning billets. Draft inspected by C.O. Bugler CHK Gee MC (Augt) Leave to England. Divine Service.	
	16th		Baths & short training	
	17th		hrs 2 SpS.	
	18th		Training. Exhibition Evans Lewis Pattern.	
	19th		Training. 1 OR Cryothorax killed. Capt 10H Roberton to England to Cooperate.	
	20th		Training. 20 OR joined from 2nd SpS.	
	21st		Training. Lieut H Cross & 2Lt L Sproat joined from 7 SpS.	
	22nd		Cleaning billets. GOC northern Div inspected billets and saw men at work. Lieut CW Smith & 2Lt P Blades joined from 7 SpS.	
	23rd		Divine Service.	

(A8904) D. D. & I., London, E.C. Wt W1771/M2931 750,000 5/17 Sch. 52 Forms/C2118/14

CONFIDENTIAL

ORIGINAL   Army Form C. 2118.

9th Bn The Durham Light Infantry
Vol XLVIII
Page 3

WAR DIARY or INTELLIGENCE SUMMARY.
(Erase heading not required.)

Instructions regarding War Diaries and Intelligence Summaries are contained in F. S. Regs., Part II. and the Staff Manual respectively. Title pages will be prepared in manuscript.

Place	Date	Hour	Summary of Events and Information	Remarks and references to Appendices
Cologne	24		Training	
	25		Training of junior NCOs under Bn M	
	26		Training. 4 Officers + 187 OR joined from 15 SB D.L.I	
	27		Training. Draft inspected by C.O. M	
	28		Training. 3 Officers + 165 ORs joined from 13th OK D.L.I. Bn commences to move out of West Cerky Kaserne & Turners reserve M	
	29		Cleaning billets - Coys at Bertha. M	
	30		Divine Service. Bn furnished a Guard of Honour to the C in C at Cologne Sn. M	
	31		Training. A Coy moves to Ehrel Barracks for work on Ehrel Rifle Range. C Coy moved into billets vacated by A Coy. M	

CONFIDENTIAL

ORIGINAL

Army Form C. 2118.

1/ 9th Bn The Durham Light Infantry
Vol XLIX

WAR DIARY
or
INTELLIGENCE SUMMARY.
(Erase heading not required.)

Instructions regarding War Diaries and Intelligence Summaries are contained in F. S. Regs., Part II. and the Staff Manual respectively. Title pages will be prepared in manuscript.

Place	Date	Hour	Summary of Events and Information	Remarks and references to Appendices
Cologne	1st		Training	
	2nd		Training	
	3rd		Training	
	4th		Training	
	5th		Training	
	6th		Baths. Cleaning billets. Coy detachment at Königsdorf relieved by A Coy M	
	7th		Divine Service M	
			Education + training. Working party 5 O.R. from B Coy / + 529 Coy RE at Marsdorf, daily except Sundays until further orders.	
	8th		Training M	
	9th		Battalion less detachment at Königsdorf Coo 3 Coy workng party moved from Hindenburg to Rhiel Barracks 13 Block Battalion	
	10th		Keep at 13 Worringer Strasse Rhiel Cologne M	
			Went on fillig trips to Rhiel and general clean up of new quarters. Furnished guard to Military Governess Headqrs Hotel Monopol Cologne M	
	11th		Education work in ranges. 150 OR tup up the Rhine by boat A	

CONFIDENTIAL

ORIGINAL

Army Form C. 2118.

WAR DIARY
or
INTELLIGENCE SUMMARY.
(Erase heading not required.)

2nd Bn. The Durham Light Infantry
Vol. XLIX (contd)

Instructions regarding War Diaries and Intelligence Summaries are contained in F. S. Regs., Part II. and the Staff Manual respectively. Title pages will be prepared in manuscript.

Place	Date	Hour	Summary of Events and Information	Remarks and references to Appendices
COLOGNE	12th		General cleaning up. Bathm range. C Coy detachment at KONIGSDORF relieved by C Coy. MS	
	13th		Divine service MS	
	14th		Education, training & baths. MS	
	15th		Training. Capt & Adjt CHR Gee VC proceeded to demobilisation MS	
	16th		Education & Training. 120 O.R.s of the Brigade left for classes fn demobilisation MS	
	17th		Training & work MS	
	18th		Easter Sunday - Divine Service MS	
	19th		General cleaning up & parades. A Coy at work on Range. C Coy detachment at KONIGSDORF relieved by A Coy MS	
	20		Divine Service. Lt-Col. G.W. Jeffreys DSO took over command of the Battn from Lt Col E.G. Arnold DSO, DCM. MS	
	21		Education. A Coy at work on the Range MS	

D. D. & L., London, E.C.
(A81041) Wt W17771/M2931 750,000 3/17 Sch. 52 Forms/C2118/14

ORIGINAL

CONFIDENTIAL

Army Form C. 2118.

3
O.C. B. The Buckinghamshire Infantry
Vol XLIX (issue)

WAR DIARY
or
INTELLIGENCE SUMMARY.
(Erase heading not required.)

Instructions regarding War Diaries and Intelligence Summaries are contained in F. S. Regs., Part II. and the Staff Manual respectively. Title pages will be prepared in manuscript.

Place	Date	Hour	Summary of Events and Information	Remarks and references to Appendices
Cologne	22		A Coy work on Range. B Coy commence work at Bridge Schemes making	
	23		Bn rest	
	24		A Coy & C Coy continue work	
	25		do	
	26		do	
	27		Divine Service	
	28		A Coy & C Coy continue work	
	29		do	
	30		do	

CONFIDENTIAL

Army Form C. 2118.

WAR DIARY
or
INTELLIGENCE SUMMARY.   9th Bn The Durham Light Infantry

Vol XLX

(Erase heading not required.)

9th BATTALION,
THE DURHAM
LIGHT INFANTRY

B 252

Instructions regarding War Diaries and Intelligence
Summaries are contained in F. S. Regs., Part II.
and the Staff Manual respectively. Title pages
will be prepared in manuscript.

Place	Date	Hour	Summary of Events and Information	Remarks and references to Appendices
Cologne	May 1st		Training	
	2nd		Training	
	3rd		Baths. Cleaning of Billets	
	4th		Divine Service. Billets inspected by Commander-in-Chief	
	5th		Training. Interviews of Divisn by G.O.C.	
	6th		Training	
	7th		Training	
	8th		Training	
	9th		Divisional Review by H.R.H. the Duke of Connaught	
	10th		Training	
	11th		Baths. Cleaning of Billets. Medical Inspection.	
	12th		Divine Service	
	13th		Training	
	14th		Training. Whole of B Coy move to Kundorf for work	

CONFIDENTIAL

Army Form C. 2118.

WAR DIARY
or
INTELLIGENCE SUMMARY.

9th Bn 1st Division Light Infantry

Vol XLA

(Erase heading not required.)

Instructions regarding War Diaries and Intelligence Summaries are contained in F. S. Regs., Part II. and the Staff Manual respectively. Title pages will be prepared in manuscript.

Place	Date	Hour	Summary of Events and Information	Remarks and references to Appendices
Cologne	15th		Training	
	16th		Training. Battalion furnish Guard of Honour to receive Marshal Foch. Lecture by Staff Capt. Empoyt Jones on "Bullet Cluster Bridge"	
	17th		Baths. Cleaning of Billets. Medical Inspection. Guard at MONOPOLE HOTEL increase to 1 Sgt. 1 Cpl. 1 men	
	18th		Divine Service. Inspection of Bne Robinson	
	19th		While of "C" Coy move to KONIGSDORF	
	20th		Training	
	21st		Training	
	22nd		Training	
	23rd		Training. "Green Diamonds" Concert Party gave concert at Entire	
	24th		Baths. Cleaning of billets	Y.M.C.A
	25.		Divine Service. Medical Inspection	
	26th		Barracks inspected by Corps Commander	

CONFIDENTIAL

Army Form C. 2118.

WAR DIARY
or
INTELLIGENCE SUMMARY. 9th Br. a/Duke of Light Infantry
(Erase heading not required.) Vol XI-X

Army Form C. 2118. 3

Place	Date	Hour	Summary of Events and Information	Remarks and references to Appendices
Cologne	27		Training	
	28		Training. Lecture by Rev R Oulass "Visit through the Russian Zones"	
	29		Training	
	30		Training	
	31		Batto Cleaning of Billets. Medical Inspection	

J.L. Jeffreys

CONFIDENTIAL

Army Form C. 2118.

9th Battalion, The Durham Light Infantry

9th Bn. The Durham Light Infantry
Vol XLVI

WAR DIARY or INTELLIGENCE SUMMARY.

(Erase heading not required.)

No. B.124 Date 6-8-19

Place	Date	Hour	Summary of Events and Information	Remarks and references to Appendices
Cologne	1st		Battalion returns to Field Barracks from LINDLAR	
	2nd		Cleaning equipment billets &c	
	3rd		Address on commemoration of the signing of Peace	
	4th		Guard of Honour furnished for Belgian Commander in Chief Army of Occupation	
	5th		Bath Inspection. Cleaning of billets	
	6th		Divine Service	
	7th		Training. Education	
	8th		Training. 2 Platoons carrying out Practices 1, 2 & 3 of the B.M.G on 25yd. gallery range	
	9th		Education	
	10th		Training	
	11th		Jury in Camp entrenched. Y. troop trains taken over by El Corps. Cyclists Section	
	12th		Bath. Kit inspection. Cleaning of billets	
	13th		Divine Service	
	14th		Training. Firing on rifle range. Education	
	15th		Education – Examination	
	16th		Training. Education	

CONFIDENTIAL

Army Form C. 2118.

WAR DIARY
or
INTELLIGENCE SUMMARY. 9th Bn. The Durham Light Infy.

(Erase heading not required.)

Instructions regarding War Diaries and Intelligence Summaries are contained in F. S. Regs. Part II. and the Staff Manual respectively. Title pages will be prepared in manuscript.

Vol. XXXI

Place	Date	Hour	Summary of Events and Information	Remarks and references to Appendices
Boulogne	16th		Training	
	18th		Evacuation Troops at Military Police Barracks & Iron Barrack from here sent	
		2.30pm	2nd Bn in this Unit	
	19th		Holiday. Day of Arrival Queuing for the Conway Race from 20 to 12 Noon	
	20th		Church Service	
	21st		Training	
	22nd		Training	
	23rd		Training Education	
	24th		Training	
	25th		Training	
	26th		Training Lecture by Mr E.B. Osborn "British Empire in history	
			Basis of the Jurisdiction Meaning of Titles	
	27th		Divine Service	
	28th		Evening Education	
	29th		Training Lecture by Captain Lindsay A.D., O.B.E., "The Romance of Geology"	
	30th		Training Education	
	31st		Training	

J.L. Jeffer
Lieut Colonel
Commdg 9th Bn. The Durham Light Infantry

CONFIDENTIAL.
Army Form C. 2118.

9th Bn. The Durham Light Infantry
VOL. XLVII

WAR DIARY
or
INTELLIGENCE SUMMARY.
(Erase heading not required.)

Instructions regarding War Diaries and Intelligence Summaries are contained in F. S. Regs., Part II. and the Staff Manual respectively. Title pages will be prepared in manuscript.

Place	Date	Hour	Summary of Events and Information	Remarks and references to Appendices
Cologne	1st		Training. Education	
	2nd		Baths, Kit Inspection, Cleaning of Billets	
	3rd		Divine Service	
	4th		Bank Holiday. Guard, Band & Bugles supplied for II Corps Intelligent Lectures	
	5th		Training - do - - do -	
	6th		Training. Education	
	7th		Divine Service of the Northern Division	
	8th		Training. Education	
	9th		Baths. Kit Inspection. Cleaning of Barracks	
	10th		Divine Service	
	11th		Training. Education	
	12th		Training	
	13th		Training. Education	
	14th		Training	

CONFIDENTIAL.
Army Form C. 2118.

2nd Bn. The Durham Light Infantry
Vol. XLXII

WAR DIARY
or
INTELLIGENCE SUMMARY.
(Erase heading not required.)

Instructions regarding War Diaries and Intelligence Summaries are contained in F.S. Regs., Part II. and the Staff Manual respectively. Title pages will be prepared in manuscript.

Place	Date	Hour	Summary of Events and Information	Remarks and references to Appendices
Bapaume	15th		Training and also trip.	
	16th		Practice Riven parade (3rd Northern Brigade). Practice Stockleys Patrol.	
	17th		Divine Service. 1 Kent. (A/Capt) J. O. Smith posted for special appointment	
	18th		Army Burial river VI Corps	
	19th		Training. Stockleys Patrol for Army Burial	
	20th		Training. Education	
	21st		Training. "	
	22nd		Training. Education	
	23rd		" also The Inspection. Cleaning of Barracks	
	24th		Divine Service	
	25th		Training. Education	
	26th		Training. "	
	27th		Training. Education	
	28th		Training. Education	
	29th		Training. Education	
	30th		Baths. Kit Inspection. Cleaning of Barracks. Lieut Colonel	
	31st		Divine Service. Commdg 2nd Bn. The Durham L.I.	

WAR DIARY or INTELLIGENCE SUMMARY
Army Form C. 2118. CONFIDENTIAL

Month: *Cologne* XLIII
9th Bn. The Durham Light Infantry

Place	Date	Hour	Summary of Events and Information	Remarks and references to Appendices
Cologne	1st		Training. Education	
	2nd		Training. Education	
	3rd		Training. Education	
	4th		Training. Lecture by Capt A.P. Hurston on "Science & History of Aviation"	
	5th		Training. Lecture & cleaning of Barracks	
	6th		Baths. Att. Relieved & cleaned H.Q. for Dispersal	
	7th		Divine Service. 54 O.Rs. to H.Q. for Dispersal	
	8th		Training. Education	
	9th		Training. Education	
	10th		Training. Education. 4 O.Rs to H.Q. for Dispersal	
	11th		Training	
	12th		Training. Education	
	13th		Baths. Kit Inspection & cleaning of Barracks	
	14th		Divine Service	
	15th		Training. Musketry Practice on Eastern Range. 16 O.Rs returned to Battn. for Discharge	

Confidential

Army Form C. 2118.

WAR DIARY
or
INTELLIGENCE SUMMARY.

(Erase heading not required.)

Instructions regarding War Diaries and Intelligence Summaries are contained in F. S. Regs., Part II. and the Staff Manual respectively. Title pages will be prepared in manuscript.

Place	Date	Hour	Summary of Events and Information	Remarks and references to Appendices
Wimereux	16th		Training. Firing on Range.	
	14th		Training. Firing on Range. 40 ORs to UK for Dispersal	
	18th		Training. Education	
	19th		Battalion Sports	
	20th		Baths. Kit Inspection & Cleaning of Billets. 24 ORs to UK for Dispersal	
	21		Church Service	
	22		Education. Recreation	
	23		Training. 20 ORs to UK for Dispersal	
	24		Training. Musketry Practice on Range	
	25		Training. Education	
	26		Baths. Kit Inspection & Cleaning of Barracks	
	27		Church Service	
	28		Training. Education	
	29		Training. Musketry Practice on Range	
	30			

29.10.19.

[signed] Lt Col
Comdg. 4th Bn the Durham L.I.

Army Form C. 2118.

WAR DIARY
or
INTELLIGENCE SUMMARY.

(Erase heading not required.)

Volume XXII

9th Bn. The Queen's Regt.

Place	Date	Hour	Summary of Events and Information	Remarks and references to Appendices
Outtersteene	1		Musketry	
	2		Training	
	3		Resolution drawn	
	4		Kit Inspection & clearing of armoury	
	5		Divine Service	
	6		Education	
	7		Training	
	8		Training	
	9		Training	
	10		Training Musketry 60 Rds to NA for Defence	
	11		Bath	
	12		Kit Inspection & clearing of billets	
	13		Divine Service – O.R. 35 NA for Offence	
			Training Musketry 80 Rds to S.N. for Defence	
	14		30 Rds to S for Defence	
	15		Training	20	

WAR DIARY
or
INTELLIGENCE SUMMARY.

Army Form C. 2118.

Place	Date	Hour	Summary of Events and Information	Remarks and references to Appendices
Ostend	16		Training & Operator	
	17		Training Operator 60 ORs to UK on Relieve	
	18		Rest till Dinner & Cleaning of Services	
	19		Church Service 25 ORs to UK on Relieve	
	20		Services	
	21		Training 128 other ranks paid to Base Ord	
	22		" "	
	23		Cleaning Barracks	
	24		Training " Op to UK on Relieve	
	25		Both Hut Inspection Cleaning of Barracks 28 ORs to UK on Amb	
	26		Divine Service	
	27		Cleaning Barracks	
	28		Training & Kit to UK on Relieve 8 Officers to Base Ord	
	29		Cleaning Service 10 Oth O up to UK on Relieve 2 Officers to	
	30		Training & Kit to UK on Relieve 2 officers to 29 in Base Ord	
	31		Cleaning Service 5 Officers to UK on Relieve 30 ORs to Base Ord	

R. Mackay

3RD DIVISION
DIVL. TROOPS

20TH BATTALION
K.R.R.C.
1918. JAN - 1918 DEC

2 DIV
To LIGHT DIVISION (formerly 2 DIV)
1 Light Bde.

Army Form C. 2118.

WAR DIARY
or
INTELLIGENCE SUMMARY.
(Erase heading not required.)

20 K.R.R.C Vol 19

Instructions regarding War Diaries and Intelligence Summaries are contained in F. S. Regs., Part II. and the Staff Manual respectively. Title pages will be prepared in manuscript.

Place	Date	Hour	Summary of Events and Information	Remarks and references to Appendices
Mory	1-1-18	8am	Training + digging trenches in damp + wet ground round huts.	
do	2-1-18	6pm	do	
do	3-1-18	6pm	do	
do	4-1-18	6pm	do	
do	5-1-18	6pm	do	
do	6-1-18	6pm	do	
do	7-1-18	6pm	do	
do	8-1-18	6pm	do	
do	9-1-18	6pm	do	
do	10-1-18	6pm	do	
do	11-1-18	6pm	do	
"	12.1.18	6pm	do	
"	13.1.18	6pm	Work on M.t Battle System under VI Corps, all Coys working half platoon each working 425 x trench dug.	
"	14.1.18	6pm	Continued work at Jn 13 Limit of defenses + W.9.W.8 trench	
"	15.1.18	6pm	Completed trench 5' deep 6'top 3' bottom	
"	16.1.18	6pm	Marked new fire trench at T.18.L.c.3.6. 130 x trench dug	
"	17.1.18	6pm	Continued work on new trench 300 x dug	
"	18.1.18	6pm	do - A Coy completed old wire front + double apron on 1st battle system erected 350 x wire	
"	19.1.19	6pm	Continued wiring 1250 x double apron fence erected	
"	20.1.18	6pm	Continued wiring 1400 x	
"	21.1.18	6pm	Continued wiring 1400 x	
"	22.1.18	6pm	Continued wiring 1200 x	
"	23.1.18	6pm	Continued wiring 1560 x	
"	24.1.18	6pm	Continued wiring 1530 x	

Army Form C. 2118.

WAR DIARY
or
INTELLIGENCE SUMMARY.

(Erase heading not required.)

Instructions regarding War Diaries and Intelligence Summaries are contained in F. S. Regs., Part II. and the Staff Manual respectively. Title pages will be prepared in manuscript.

Stamp: 20TH BN KINGS ROYAL RIFLE CORPS ORDERLY ROOM 1888

Place	Date	Hour	Summary of Events and Information	Remarks and references to Appendices
MORY	25.1.18	6pm	Continued work on third belt of double apron fence on 1st battle system 136 S. eyes.	
"	26.1.18	6pm	Continued wiring on first battle system. 800' C & B. Coy on second line system 800 x	
"	27.1.18	6pm	C & B. Coy continued wiring second system. 1200 x erected. A & D. Coys constructed	
			wire on first battle system. 200 x erected & completed the work, consisting of one	
			belt the whole length of divisional front.	
HENIN	28.1.18	6pm	B. Coy & H.Q. moved to HENIN. A & C Coys to CROISILLE. D. Coy to NEUVILLE VITASSE	
"	29.1.18	6pm	All companys visited & improved billets	
"	30.1.18	6pm	A Coy erected 250 x standard apron fence on front line a U.N.A.7. Improvements & H37.	
			Support line at O.25.d.L. near Dugout #13.	
			B. Coy. " 200 x " " " from NELLY AVENUE to 50 x N of SENSEE RIVER.	
			C. Coy. " 600 x " " " in front of SOUTHERN AVENUE W of GUEMAPPE	
			D. Coy. " 410 x " " "	
"	31.1.18	6pm	A. Coy (Continued) work on front line 250 x erected. B. Coy continued on support	
			line 200 x erected. C. Coy continued on SENSEE defences 400 x erected. D. Coy	
			erected 300 x entanglement consisting of two double apron fences 6' apart with	
			loose wire between - 15' in front of existing wire from about N.19.B.1.9 to COJEUL R.R.	

Russell Martin Lt Col
Comdg. xx K.R.R.C.

WAR DIARY or INTELLIGENCE SUMMARY

Army Form C. 2118.

2nd K.R.R.C.
21 January 1918

Place	Date	Hour	Summary of Events and Information	Remarks and references to Appendices
HENIN	1.2.18	6pm	A Coy erected 200x double apron fence from U.14.a.6.9.6 U.C.3.2. in front of front line and G.11.B.y.o.7.0.o. - B. Coy erected 200x of wire fences on g.6 Bde front, on subsidiary fence in front of BULLFINCH SUPPORT - C Coy wiring SENSÉE VALLEY defences from NELLY AVENUE working N. D Coy working in GUÉMAPPE defences from end of PANTHER TRENCH working N.	
do	2.2.18	6pm	All companies continued work as for 1.2.18.	
do	3.2.18	6pm	A Coy continued wiring front line. B. Coy started wiring front line & commencing at post G.11.B. switch S, C + D Coys continued work as for 3.2.18.	
do	4.2.18	6pm	All Coys continued work as for 4.2.18.	
do	5.2.18	6pm	All Coys continued work as for 5.2.18. III Coy comp'ld U.6.2 GUÉMAPPE defences —	
do	6.2.18	6pm	A.B.C. Coys continued as for 6.2.18. D Coy started wiring BLUE LINE, starting at GORDON AVENUE & working S.	
do	7.2.18	6pm	All Coys continued working as for 7.2.18.	
do	8.2.18	6pm	A.B & C Coys continued work as for 8.2.18. D Coy continued work as on 8.2.18 wiring 3 rows Bsa fence between Coy ws.	
do	9.2.18	6pm	A B + C Coys continued work as on 9.2.18. D Coy wiring in SKIKKAR avenue.	
do	10.2.18	6pm	A B + C + D Coys continued work as on 10.2.18.	
do	11.2.18	6pm	A B + C + D Coys continued work as on 11.2.18. D Coy commenced wiring BISON RESERVE working from Rotten Row.	
do	12.2.18	6pm	A.B + C Coys continued work as on 12.2.18 except B. Coy who commenced wiring from ROTTEN ROW.	
do	13.2.18	6pm	All Coys continued work as on 0S1d 2-3. B Coy wired in front of Bdo Stop trenches along Tunnel Trench to SWIFT R. & continued wiring along SWIFT R. Trench.	
do	14.2.18	6pm	A. C + D Coys continued work as for 13-2-18.	
do	15.2.18	6pm	A C + D Coys continued work as for 14-2-18. B " " " " "	
do	16.2.18	6pm	All Coys continued wiring as for 15.2.18.	
do	17.2.18	6pm	All Coys continued wiring as in 16.2.18. TUNNEL TRENCH. B Coy continued wiring from Nelis SENSÉE RIVER in front of	
do	19.2.18	6pm	A Coy wired 300x sock off SENSÉE River hindered by enemy trench mortar fire. C Coy wired HOOK SENSÉE RESERVE — D Coy wired RB by permission of O.C. 76th Inf Bde.	

Army Form C. 2118.

WAR DIARY
or
INTELLIGENCE SUMMARY.

(Erase heading not required.)

Instructions regarding War Diaries and Intelligence Summaries are contained in F. S. Regs., Part II. and the Staff Manual respectively. Title pages will be prepared in manuscript.

Place	Date	Hour	Summary of Events and Information	Remarks and references to Appendices
HENIN.	19.2.18	6 p.m.	A Coy continued driving front line 300× drive erected from CROISILLES FONTAINE road to about U.7.d.8.9. B/Coy erected 250× drive along SWIFT SUPPORT - C Coy erected double apron fence along SENSEE AVENUE - D Coy erected 300× drive on trench line along KESTREL RESERVE - C Coy erected 200× drive in front of NELLY + JANET RESERVE - B Coy 300× drive in front of LONGRETE RESERVE. C Coy 300× drive along HIND SUPPORT - D Coy 300× drive in continuation of last night's work.	
"	20.2.18	6 p.m.	All Coys continued work as for 20 inst.	
"	21.2.18	6 p.m.	All Coys continued work as for 21.2.18.	
"	22.2.18	6 p.m.	A. Coy 300× in front of NELLY and BURGH SUPPORT. B Coy 350× in front of FIRST AVENUE + QUERZON - C. Coy 300× along FAULKNER. D Coy 3 belts of 150 yds in front of NEW GANET RESERVE -	
"	23.2.18	6 p.m.	All Coys continued work, as for 23.2.18 —	
"	24.2.18	6 p.m.	A.B.D. Coys continued work as for 24.2.18. C Coy wired 300× of LINCOLN RESERVE —	
"	25.2.18	6 p.m.	D Coy erected 135× each of three belts in front of KEY RESERVE — A. B. C continued wiring as 25.2.18.	
"	26.2.18	6 p.m.	Reorganized new views (established) to NEUVILLE VITASSE. A Coy to HENIN - D Coy broken up and absorbed into A. B. + C Coys	
"	27.2.18	6 p.m.	A Coy erected 500× drive on N side of SHAFT TRENCH along BLUE LINE - B Coy 500× along EGRET TRENCH. C Coy continued 500× drive in front of KEY, SOUTHERN and CAVALRY TRENCHES to S. side of CAMBRAI Rd.	

Russell M. Bastio
Bdr
Comy. XX RRRE

3rd Divisional Troops

20th BATTALION

K. R. R. C. (Pioneers)

MARCH 1918

Army Form C. 2118.

20th K.R.R.C.
(Pioneers)

WAR DIARY
or
INTELLIGENCE SUMMARY.
(Erase heading not required.)

Instructions regarding War Diaries and Intelligence Summaries are contained in F. S. Regs., Part II. and the Staff Manual respectively. Title pages will be prepared in manuscript.

Place	Date	Hour	Summary of Events and Information	Remarks and references to Appendices
HENIN	1/3/18	6pm	A Coy erected 300ˣ wire in front of GREY TRENCH. B Coy 500ˣ along EGRET - C Coy 500ˣ along KESTREL	
"	2.3.18	6pm	All Coys continued wiring. 1300ˣ double apron fence erected	
"	3.3.18	6pm	All Coys continued wiring. 1500ˣ double apron fence erected	
"	4.3.18	6pm	A Coy erected 500ˣ wire for BROWN SUPPORT. B Coy erected 500ˣ along (cont⁴?) RESERVE & FOSTER	
"	5.3.18	6pm	C Coy started down across ROUEIL VALLEY	
"	6.2.18	6pm	A Coy continued 500ˣ wire. B Coy (continued) 400ˣ wire along MALLARD - C Coy (continued) down	
"	7.3.18	6pm	A Coy erected 660ˣ between CROISILLES - HEMINEL Road & GREY TRENCH. B Coy erected 500ˣ wire along MALLARD & GANNET RESERVE - C Coy completed down across ROUEIL VALLEY -	
"	8.3.18	6pm	A+B Coys All wire erected. GREY ST & FIRST AVENUE - 5 & 1/2 hr 110ˣ F C Coy A Coy erected 500ˣ double apron fence along NEW BUZZARD - 36 1/2 ft 110ˣ F	
"	9.3.18	6pm	A.B.+C Coy (continued) last night's work, erected 1200ˣ wire. Double apron fence	
"	10.3.18	6pm	A.B.+C Coy (continued) last night's work. erected 1400ˣ double apron fence	
"	11.3.19	6pm	A.B.+C Coy (continued) last night's work. erected 1030ˣ double apron fence -	
"	12.3.18	6pm	A.B. TCy completed burry the dump. 140 3 belts of double apron fence, ready 2960 yds.	
"	13.3.18	6pm	A.B.C.Cy ?? black and ?? ?? & ?? & ?? visits in pavilion	
"	14.3.18	6pm	A+B Coy worked on New French railway ?? & different passes & place. 50 knife visits in park	
"	15.3.18	6pm	C Coy fix'd 500ˣ wire in front of BUCK RESERVE & SHIKKAR AVENUE	
"	16.3.18	6pm	All Coys continued work on the PM 24.3.18.	
"	17.3.18	6pm	All Coys continued work as before. 18.3.18. A Coy revetted fire step & laid duck boards - C Coy erected ?	
"	18.3.18	6pm	A+B. Coy demolished NEW TRENAH from foundations to dark & all & work	
"			A+B. Coy worked on HOUSE L ABREN - NEW TRENCH & GREY ST. deepened & widened & put in	
"	19.3.18	6pm	fire bays. C Coy continued wiring from KESTRAL to BUCK RESERVE.	
"			B Coy (new trees) worked Ahrent, ATCH. C. Coy (A) 500ˣ wire on S.E. side of BROWN SUPPORT.	
"	20.3.19	6pm	A Coy completed wiring BROWN SUPPORT. B Coy works on new tunnel from KESTRAL AVENUE started their C Coy worked on NEW TRENCH at northern end. It fuck	

A5834 Wt. W4973/M687 750,000 8/16 D. D. & L. Ltd. Form/C.2118/13.

WAR DIARY or INTELLIGENCE SUMMARY

Army Form C. 2118.

Place	Date	Hour	Summary of Events and Information	Remarks and references to Appendices
HENIN	21.3.18	6 pm	A.B.C Coys work on new trench from NEUTRAL AVENUE to LION SUPPORT, trench 4 complete [to] 300 x 24 inches, 150 ft. 3' deep —	
NEUVILLE VITASSE	22.3.18	6 pm	Battalion stood to at 5 am. Very heavy shelling all day. 11.30 am orders received to send two Coys to support 9th Brigade. These Coys held HIND SUPPORT until orders to withdraw at 3 pm. Remaining 2 Coys & HQ continued to come through at the Div on the right of HENIN-BOISLEUX Rd had broken — Enemy patrols were seen 500 yds from east of hill. So decided to withdraw headquarters to	
WAILLY	23.3.18	6 pm	NEUVILLE VITASSE. [illegible] arrived at night H.Q. Coy & support 9 Brigade. At 7 pm 2 of our Coys went forward from stn[?] to take headquarters & Coy to support 9 Brigade. Brigade HQ at 8.30, men took up position in reserve trench. At 11.30, 12.30 am received orders from Brigade to withdraw Brigade to withdraw down shaft trench. (Coy [illegible] to be the last to leave — this was carried out successfully) Brigade & Trenches[?] were evacuated by 4.30 am. Battalion moved into Hd[?] at NORTHUMBERLAND LINES. At 6.30 am orders received at 10.30 am to move to WAILLY. On the night of 22nd at 8 pm the 2nd SHINN Scout [illegible] a party to recover Kit etc that we were compelled to leave in HENIN Rd. This was successfully carried out, in spite of the fact that the enemy was only 500 yards of the line — Even full[?] kit[?] was left — no transport is a place of safety.	
BELLACOURT	24.3.18	6 pm	[illegible] detached by 1 Div [illegible] 2nd transport at 12.30 pm with headquarters & three platoons — 3 Coys less 3 platoons moved to [illegible] area to work on PURPLE LINE — Commenced digging & wiring	
"	25.3.18	6 pm	All Coys at work on PURPLE LINE	
"	26.3.18	6 pm	" " " PURPLE LINE	
"	27.3.18	6 pm	(Continued) Work on PURPLE LINE. Division made a splendid effort & last night having finished their first 1800 x task did so with the issue of completing the wire	
"	28.3.18	6 pm	Orders to take up position in the PURPLE LINE, with Battalion & 3 Coys of Ret's. A Co's 200 yards, 20 WIRKE on left. 3 Platoons on right, ammunition places in front. Support line by 9 pm [illegible] the disposing of our Ret[?] trench ammunition at mess —	
"	29.3.18	6 pm	On night of 28 at 11.30 Brig rec'd that the CANADIAN BRIGADES would relieve us. This division would stand to. Not completed until 5.30 pm. The Battalion moved back to BELLACOURT.	

Army Form C. 2118.

WAR DIARY
or
INTELLIGENCE SUMMARY.
(Erase heading not required.)

Instructions regarding War Diaries and Intelligence Summaries are contained in F. S. Regs., Part II. and the Staff Manual respectively. Title pages will be prepared in manuscript.

Place	Date	Hour	Summary of Events and Information	Remarks and references to Appendices
SUS. ST. LEDGER	30.3.19	6/pm	Night of 29th at 6.30 p.m. moved from BELLACOURT to BOUY arriving at 9.30 p.m. 12 noon 30/3 moved from BOUY to SUS ST LEDGER arriving at 4 p.m. under orders of 8th Brigade.	
"	31.3.19	6/pm	Spent the day at SUS. ST LEDGER. Obtained a clean change for men & took usual hot baths. B70 did the best they could to put the men warm at their billets - seniors & juniors tomorrow to AUCHEL AREA	Russell Martin Lt. Col.

3rd Division PIONEERS)

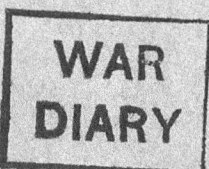

20th BATTALION

KINGS ROYAL RIFLE CORPS

(Pioneers))

A P R I L 1 9 1 8

20TH K.R.R.C. (Pioneers)

April 1918

Army Form C. 2118.

WAR DIARY
or
INTELLIGENCE SUMMARY.
(Erase heading not required.)

Instructions regarding War Diaries and Intelligence Summaries are contained in F.S. Regs., Part II. and the Staff Manual respectively. Title pages will be prepared in manuscript.

Place	Date	Hour	Summary of Events and Information	Remarks and references to Appendices
BRUAY	1.4.18	6pm	The battalion moved by motor buses to BRUAY arriving at 3.30pm. Transport moved by road via H the Major —	
"	2.4.18	6pm	Battalion training commenced, all the men attended Gas talks. Transport arrived at 3pm —	
"	3.4.18	6pm	Training continued. Gunner & Platoon drill & Musketry	
LES BREVEY	4.4.18	6pm	Battalion moved at 8.45am to LES BREVEY arriving 12.45pm	
"	5.4.18	6pm	100 men of B+C Coys worked on Corps Defences Remainder of battalion training	
"	6.4.18	6pm	100 men of A+B+C Coy worked on Corps Defences. Remainder of battalion training	
"	7.4.18	6pm	Lock & Karring continued. 56 men of B+C+D Coys passed C.E. remainder training	
"	8.4.18	6pm	Lock & training continued as for 7 N.H.	
"	9.4.18	6pm	Lock & training continued as for 7 N.H.	
"	10.4.18	6pm	Lock & training continued as for 7 N.H.	
LA BOURSE	11.4.18	6pm	Battalion moved to LABOURSE arriving at 1.30pm. Orders received to move to GONNEHEM	
GONNEHEM	12.4.18	6pm	Battalion marched to BETHUNE road & embussed for GONNEHEM at 11.30pm the night of 11 4.18 arriving at GONNEHEM at 4am — Reconnaissance & Decided on strong points & scheme of defence	
"	13.4.18	6pm	Battalion busy digging S.W. of LA BASSE CANAL	
CHOQUES	14.4.18	6pm	Battalion continued digging work last night & moved to CHOQUES — arriving CHOQUES at 1pm —	
"	15.4.18	6pm	A + B Coy supplied 1250* ratns for on divisional forms	
"	16.4.18	6pm	Battalion found 1900* ratns on front from LA BASSE CANAL Eastward to X 15 a.5.0.	
"	17.4.18	6pm	Battalion supplied 2070* ratns on Bridge heads in continuation of work	
"	18.4.18	6pm	A Coy found 800* ratns on SEVELINGHE SUPPORT LINE — B Coy supplied 900* ratns on substitutions from W.18.c.95.50. to W.18.d.2.8. also round work at W.18.a.6.1. C Coy supplied 450* ratns in vicinity of Rue de Bois, full of W/light with some & places obstacles & trip wires at edge of wood.	
"	19.4.18	6pm	Battalion [continued work] ...	
"	20.4.18	6pm	...	
"	21.4.18	6pm	A Coy ... CANAL DE LA LAWE ...	
"	22.4.18	6pm	A Coy duty 50* ... CANAL DE LA LAWE — ...	
"	23.4.18	6pm	A Coy duty ... CANAL DE LA LAWE — B Coy ...	
"	24.4.18	6pm	B Coy ... PERTH LINE	
"	25.4.18	6pm	Battalion ...	
"	26.4.18	6pm	A & C Coys ... PERTH LINE	
"	27.4.18	6pm	A + C Coys Infy supplied 5 posts ... SE of VINGES — PIONEER LINE — B.C ...	

WAR DIARY
or
INTELLIGENCE SUMMARY.
(Erase heading not required.)

Army Form C. 2118.

Instructions regarding War Diaries and Intelligence Summaries are contained in F. S. Regs., Part II. and the Staff Manual respectively. Title pages will be prepared in manuscript.

Place	Date	Hour	Summary of Events and Information	Remarks and references to Appendices
RHODES	28.4.19	6pm	A Coy. ran 50 yds deep 100' parapet trench N.W. 15 a 7.3. 9 to new foot Savewood trench in W.16.a.0.1. & 50 x 4'. N. 16.a.2.5. communicating with Lancaster Line. B Coy plus 53 men of 158 E. completed apron fence from W.16.c.6.7. 8.7.2.3. at N.J. 2.5.2. & front opening W.16.c.2.a. & wired 1200 double apron fence for Shropshire Line & further 500 yds Shropshire line - A Coy worm killed.	
"	29.4.19	6pm		
-	30.4.19	6pm	2nd Lieut Arnwood finish the construction of Lancaster Line & did important work in Suffolk Trench on B Coy front. 13 Coy erected 650 x double apron fence in W.16 a 8.3. & dip drawn for in 15.a.9.h. 2nd Rifleman E. Bloomson awarded the Military Medal for conspicuous bravery contra. battle Ath Jan -	Russell Brooke Lt Col comm X.X.R.C.

20th K.R.R.C.

Army Form C. 2118

WAR DIARY or INTELLIGENCE SUMMARY
(Erase heading not required.)

Vol 23

Place	Date	Hour	Summary of Events and Information	Remarks and references to Appendices
CHOCQUES	1.5.18	6pm	All companys digging harassed his branch on PIONEER LINE	
"	2.5.18	6pm	A Coy dug 100x100' belts on SUFFOLK SWITCH. C Coy dug two circular belts - B Coy erected 800' wire	
"	3.5.18	6pm	A + B Coy erected 1500 x double abvis fence in honeycomb of SUFFOLK TRENCH. C Coy dug 5 small half B.H.Q continuation of SUFFOLK SWITCH	
"	4.5.18	6pm	A Coy erected 800x double abvis fence in front of SUFFOLK LINE. B + C comp[letes] digging of PIONEER TRENCH	
"	5.5.18	6pm	A Coy erected 800x double abvis fence on SUFFOLK LINE. B Coy cont. C Coy digging belts in SUFFOLK SWITCH	
"	6.5.18	6pm	A Coy continued during SUFFOLK LINE. B Coy erected 550x wire from SUFFOLK LINE to CANAL. C Coy contin. digging belts in SUFFOLK SWITCH	
"	7.5.18	6pm	A + B Coy erected 1400x double abvis fence in SUFFOLK LINE. C Coy working on Brigade H.Q.	
"	8.5.18	6pm	A + B Coy continued during. C Coy continued on Brigade H.Q.	
"	9.5.18	6pm	A Coy dug two belts of 100x each in LANCASTER LINE	
"	10.5.18	6pm	A Coy worked on Brigade H.Q. (cont. belts) erection of four shelters. A + B Coy wiring	
"	11.5.18	6pm	C Coy continued work on Brigade H.Q. A + C Coys wiring	
"	12.5.18	6pm	A Coy erected 700x double abvis fence in front of PIONEER TRENCH. B Coy erected 550x wire from R. Front FARM to CANAL - SOT ANELETTE - C Coy continued work on Brigade H.Q.	
"	13.5.18	6pm	A Coy day work in SUFFOLK SUPPORT. B Coy erected 700 x wire in front of LANCASTER LINE. C Coy continued work on Brigade H.Q.	
"	14.5.18	6pm	A Coy dug 325x harassed branch on SUFFOLK SUPPORT. B Coy continued 700 wire on LANCASTER LINE. C Coy continued on Brigade H.Q.	
"	15.5.18	6pm	All Coys digging branch on March defences - W of LAWE RIVER -	
"	16.5.18	6pm	continued that night to 3 back.	
"	17.5.18	6pm	A + C Coy continued. B Coy erected 800x wire in front of belts	
"	18.5.18	6pm	A Coy dug 260x harassed branch connected up LANCASTER LINE - B Coy erected 800x wire. C.P. dug new belts to SUFFOLK SWITCH	
"	19.5.18	6pm	A Coy dug 230x harassed branch in W.K.C. B Coy erected 800x double abvis fence in LANCASTER LINE. C Coy continued revetting tranks traverse breastworks	
"	20.5.18	6pm	A Coy continued revetting traverse breastworks. B Coy on same branch working to top Reserve branch + connected will belts of distributed works. C Coy revetting + breastworks in BETHUNE SWITCH	

Army Form C.2118.

WAR DIARY
or
INTELLIGENCE SUMMARY.
(Erase heading not required.)

Instructions regarding War Diaries and Intelligence Summaries are contained in F.S. Regs., Part II. and the Staff Manual respectively. Title pages will be prepared in manuscript.

Place	Date	Hour	Summary of Events and Information	Remarks and references to Appendices
CHOCQUES	21.5.18	6pm	A + B Coy dug support trench 400x + improved existing trench from CANAL South at X 13.6.9.4 towards X 13.6.45. C Coy revetting existing posts.	
"	22.5.18	6pm	A + B Coy continued work on new trench. Building up parapet & parados. C Coy sorting balls of wire in front.	
"	23.6.18	6pm	A Coy completed trench worked on last night. B + C Coys dug 700x towards trench Ln X 13.a + 6.	
"	24.5.18	6pm	All Coys continued work on new trench. B Coy starting jct LA BASSEE CANAL & working to the right.	
"	25.5.18	6pm	All Coys continued work on new support trench, digging new parts & revetting.	
"	26.5.18	6pm	Continued work as for 25.5.18.	
"	27.5.18	6pm	Battn. manning future line.	
"	28.5.18	6pm	Continued work on new trench as for 26.5.18.	
"	29.5.18	6pm	" " " 28.5.18	
"	30.5.18	6pm	" " " 29.5.18	
"	31.5.18	6pm	All Coys continued work on new support line, digging new trench & revetting firebays.	

Chas. W. Martin
Lt.
Comg. XX K.R.R.C

20th. (S) BATTALION KING'S ROYAL RIFLE CORPS. (PIONEERS)

S E C R E T

ACTION IN CASE OF ATTACK.

1. In the event of the Division being forced to withdraw from its present position, it would withdraw fighting to successive lines of defence.

2. It may be assumed that three Infantry Brigades of approximately equal strength are available for defence of these lines, each line being held by three Infantry Brigades in line, each Brigade being disposed with two Battalions in line, with one Battalion in reserve.

3. The frontages which would be allotted to Brigades are indicated on the accompanying map by the boundaries between Brigades.

4. The 20th. K.R.R.C. will be prepared to man as a nucleus garrison BETHUNE RETRENCHMENT - BETHUNE SWITCH - CHOCQUES LINE - CLARENCE SWITCH.
   This nucleus garrison will indicate to the troops falling back the positions of lines upon which they will reform and continue the fight.

5. These lines will be reconnoitred by all Officers in the Battalion and the completion of same will be reported to Orderly Room. The whole of the lines must be reconnoitred, as well as portions particularly mentioned in para. 6.

6. The following is a brief description of the various lines of defences.

(a) BETHUNE RETRENCHMENT. Consists of a front and support line, the front line being a series of unconnected Posts.

(b) CHOCQUES LINE AND CLARENCE SWITCH. The former consists of a front and support line of breastwork and trench. The latter runs along the West bank of the Clarence River. The Northern portion only has been constructed, but the bank itself is defensible.

(c) BETHUNE SWITCH. Consists of a front, support and reserve lines, and connects our front system of trenches with the BETHUNE RETRENCHMENT. It is designed to protect the right flank of the left Brigade, and to cover the withdrawal of the right Brigade across the LA BASSEE CANAL in case of necessity, should the enemy succeed in gaining BETHUNE as a result of an attack from the East.
   The front line consists of a series of posts.
   The support and reserve lines have not yet been constructed, but defensible positions can be found along the railway embankment

7. Lewis Gun Positions. Suitable Lewis Gun positions will be found at the following places :-

BETHUNE RETRENCHMENT.	CHOCQUES LINE AND CLARENCE SWITCH.	BETHUNE SWITCH.
E.10.a.45.00	E.9.d.95.40	E.5.a.40.65
E.4.a.05.55	E.9.d.55.55	E.5.a.15.65
W.15.b.10.90	E.9.d.15.30	E.4.b.10.40
W.15.b.00.30	E.3.b.00.60	W.23.b.70.00
W.15.d.70.90	E.9.c.00.95	W.20.c.10.50
	E.3.d.60.20	W.27.d.00.55
	E.3.b.60.30	
	E.3.b.25.90	
	W.55.d.20.60	
	W.25.a.00.10	

Although it is not possible to forecast the turn of events, O.C. Coys. must be prepared for every contingency, and should be thoroughly acquainted with the lines which they may be called upon to defend.

8. O.C. Coys. will be responsible for preventing any retiring troops from crossing the line that they are garrisoning.

All stragglers will be collected, reformed, and will reinforce the line being held under the Command of the Senior Officer on the spot.

If the situation demands, Coys. with their stragglers reinforcements will fight it out on these lines.

9. The probable situation which may arise can be considered in three phases :-

(a) Should the enemy break through from the East and hold BETHUNE. In this event Coys. would be disposed as under :-

"A" Coy. will hold from Railway in W.27.a. along BETHUNE RETRENCHMENT to Railway in E.3.d. and will hold the Western post of BETHUNE SWITCH in E.3.d.

"B" Coy. will hold the line of posts of BETHUNE SWITCH connecting up with "A" Coy. on the right, and extending to the LA BASSEE CANAL at E.5.a.5.6.

"C" Coy. will hold the remainder of BETHUNE SWITCH from LA BASSEE CANAL inclusive to the junction of DUNBARTON LINE with the CANAL DE LA LAWE at W.30.a.1.6.

(b) Should the enemy break through and succeed in capturing the LA BASSEE CANAL North of BETHUNE.

"B" Coy. will hold the frontline of BETHUNE RETRENCHMENT from HINGES - OBLINGHEM Road at W.15.d.6.4. to the Railway at W.27.a.8.2. inclusive.

"A" Coy. will hold BETHUNE RETRENCHMENT from Railway at W.27.a.8.2. to Railway in E.3.d. inclusive.

"C" Coy. will hold remainder of BETHUNE RETRENCHMENT to the LA BREET River in E.10.c.

(c) Should the enemy break through on the whole front and the Battalion are ordered to occupy the CHOCQUES LINE and CLARENCE SWITCH.

"B" Coy. will occupy the CLARENCE SWITCH and CHOCQUES LINE from the N.-Divisional Boundary at W.18.c.6.1. to the Railway line at W.25.a.7.1.

"A" Coy. will occupy the CHOCQUES LINE from the Railway line inclusive to the CHOCQUES - ANNEZIN Road at E.3.c.10.25.

"C" Coy. will occupy the CHOCQUES LINE from Road at E.3.c.10.25. to Southern Divisional Boundary at E.10.c.1.5.

9. O.C. Coys. will mark down possible positions of Coy. H.Q. for each phase.

Battalion Headquarters will remain at present Billet.

10. The map mentioned in para. 3 is being circulated to Coys.

Copies to :-
COMMANDING OFFICER.
2nd. in COMMAND.
O.C. "A" Coy.
O.C. "B" Coy.
O.C. "C" Coy.
Transport Officer.
War Diary.
FILE.

Capt. Agincourt
20th KRRC

ADDENDUM No. 1 to D.104
ACTION IN CASE OF ATTACK.

1. "G" Special Coy. R.E. have been placed at the disposal of the Battalion to assist in manning, as a nucleus garrison, BETHUNE RETRENCHMENT - BETHUNE SWITCH - CHOCQUES LINE & CLARENCE SWITCH.

2. They will be alloted to Coys. as under, and will come under the orders of the O.C. Coy. concerned.

"A" Coy. No. 55 Section "G" Special Coy. R.E. and Lewis Gun with team. Approximate strength - 1 Officer, 2 Sergeants and 24 Other Ranks.

"B" Coy. No. 33 and 34 Sections. Approximate strength - 2 Officers, 2 Sergeants and 34 Other Ranks.

"C" Coy. No. 31 and 32 Sections. Approximate strength - 2 Officers, 2 Sergeants and 18 Other Ranks.

3. O.C. "G" Special Coy. R.E. will arrange for Section Officers to reconnoitre the areas alloted to Coys. to which their Sections will be attached, as laid down in para. 9 of D.104, as early as possible, and for them to get in touch with Coy. Commanders at CHOCQUES.

4. In the event of the Division issuing orders for the 20th. K.R.R.C. and "G" Special Coy. R.E. to "Stand By", all will be prepared to move at 10 minutes notice.

5. When the order "Move Off" is given, O.C. "G" Special Coy. R.E. will move forward, and will be accomodated at the Headquarters of the 20th. K.R.R.C. at CHOCQUES.
   He will be accompanied by 6 Runners.

6. When Coys. move forward to occupy one of the trench systems, O.C. "G" Special Coy. R.E. will arrange to have the rations of his Coy. delivered at the Battalion Q.M. Stores of the 20th. K.R.R.C.
They could then be distributed from there with the rations of the Coy. to which Sections are attached.

T.F.Funnell
Capt. & Adjutant.
The Kings Royal Rifle Corps.
20th. (S) Bn. (Pioneers).

Field.
25/5/18.

Copies to :-   COMMANDING OFFICER.   O.C. Transport.
               2nd. in COMMAND.   O.C. "G" Special Coy. R.E.
               O.C. "A" Coy.   3rd. DIVISION "G" (for information).
               O.C. "B" Coy.   WAR DIARY.
               O.C. "C" Coy.   File.

20th. (S) BATTALION KINGS ROYAL RIFLE CORPS. (PIONEERS).

Reference D.104 of 24th. instant, a practice manning of the Defence Lines will be carried out tonight, May 26th./27th.

All ranks will wear Fighting Kit. N.C.O.s and men will carry 120 rounds of ammunition. Water bottles will be filled and Iron Rations will be carried. All picks and shovels on Coys. charge will be carried.

O.C. Transport will send up 2 Limbers per Coy. for conveyance of Lewis Guns, ammunition and reserve ammunition, immediately on receipt of these orders. They will be loaded and stand by at Coy. H.Qrs.

O.C. Coys. will send in their disposition in the line immediately they are taken up.

The probable Line to be occupied will be the CLARENCE RIVER – CHOCQUES LINE with forward Posts in the BETHUNE RETRENCHMENT. Coys. will be prepared to move at 10 minutes notice from 5 p.m. tonight.

Capt. & Adjutant.
The Kings Royal Rifle Corps.
20th. (S) Bn. (Pioneers).

Field.
26/5/1918.

Copies to :-   COMMANDING OFFICER.   O.C. "C" Coy.
               2nd. in COMMAND.   O.C. Transport.
               O.C. "A" Coy.   O.C. "G" Special Coy. R.E.
               O.C. "B" Coy.   FILE.

20th. (S) BATTALION KINGS ROYAL RIFLE CORPS. (PIONEERS).

Reference ADDENDUM No. 1 to D.104 of todays date.

<u>Para. 2.</u> for No. 33 and 34 Sections.   Approximate strength – 2 Officers, 2 Sergeants and 34 other Ranks.
Read 2 Officers, 4 Sergeants and 54 Other Ranks.

for No. 31 and 32 Sections.   Approximate strength – 2 Officers, 2 Sergeants and 18 Other Ranks.
Read 2 Officers, 4 Sergeants and 36 Other Ranks.

Capt. & Adjutant.
The Kings Royal Rifle Corps.
20th. (S) Bn. (Pioneers).

Field.
20/5/1918.

Copies to :-   COMMANDING OFFICER.   O.C. "C" Coy.
2nd. in COMMAND   O.C. Transport.
O.C. "A" Coy.   FILE
O.C. "B" Coy.

WAR DIARY or INTELLIGENCE SUMMARY

Army Form C. 2118.

20 K.R.R.C. Vol 24

Place	Date	Hour	Summary of Events and Information	Remarks and references to Appendices
CHOCQUES	1.6.18	6pm	Battalion (less (L.M. gun) revetting ABERDEEN LINE in W.18 c.v.d.	
MAKEQUET	2.6.18	6pm	H.Q. moved to MAKEQUET. C Coy of DUNBARTON LINE. Work continued as fr 1.6.18.	
"	3.6.18	6pm	Continued work on ABERDEEN LINE.	
"	4.6.18	6pm	A + B Coy continued revetting ABERDEEN. C Coy started a new trench at LOCON Rd.	
"	5.6.18	6pm	A + B Coy day work Fauvil trench in GORDON LINE. C Coy continued moving ABERDEEN.	
"	6.6.18	6pm	A. B. + C Coys continued work as fr 5.6.18.	
"	7.6.18	6pm	A. B. C Coys continued work as fr 6.6.18.	
"	8.6.18	6pm	A. B. + C Coys continued work as fr 7.6.18.	
"	9.6.18	6pm	Work continued.	
"	10.6.18	6pm	A + B Coys continued work improving GORDON LINE. C Coy completed new 2 bellis in front	
"	11.6.18	6pm	of ABERDEEN LINE from LA BASSE to KANE CANALS.	
"	12.6.18	6pm	A + B Coys continued work in GORDON LINE. C (By mov) back to ANNEZIN.	
"	13.6.18	6pm	3rd CABLE TRENCH from W.16.a.8.8 to W.16.c.13.6. C Coy started 500x new cable trench a w.18.a	
"	14.6.18	6pm	A Coy deepening & connecting up GORDON LINE. B Coy continued cable trench & completed names.	
"	15.6.18	6pm	C Coy completed div K EDINBURGH LINE - 600x double apron fence.	
"	16.6.18	6pm	A. B. + C Coys all continued work on improving GORDON LINE.	
"	17.6.18	6pm	N/f.D. 14/15 Division advanced its line all Coys tasked - NEW ABERDEEN LINE	
"	18.6.18	6pm	All Coys deepening slope in front of lines & quickness NEDINBURGH LINE from PARK LANE to storm at	
"	19.6.18	6pm	W.17.6.95.95. - Too belts of wire erected - work was greatly hindered by L.G. shell + M.G. /M.S.	
"	20.6.18	6pm	C.O.C. has the battalion a mile/h. Yet.	
"	21.6.18	6pm	A. B Coy deepening Fauvil trench & communication posts to ABERDEEN LINE.	
"	22.6.18	6pm	All Coys continued work in ABERDEEN LINE.	
"	23.6.19	6pm	Continued work in ABERDEEN LINE.	
"	24.6.18	6pm	A & C Coy continued work on ABERDEEN LINE.	
"	25.6.18	6pm	A plus 40 N.C.O.'s meet A3 Coy continued work on GORDON LINE from about W.16.b.20.55. C Coy erected 500 meters belt from about W.10.d.70.70 K about	
"	26.6.18	6Pm	B Coy widened 600 mtre on BLACK LINE from about W.H.b.20.55 C Coy rested. A Coy rested	
"	27.6.18	6Pm	W.H.C.25.70 also strengthened line on GORDON LINE. A Coy rested	
"	"	6Pm	A Coy widened 600 mtre and lined Fells from W.H.a.0.5 to LA PANNERIE ROAD W.H.C.3.A. B Coy rested 600 mtre on BLACK LINE +	
"	"	6Pm	improved ABERDEEN TRENCH from W.H.A.25.70 towards FLEET STREET. C Coy improved & brought up 15 standard opp FLEET S. C	
"	28.6.18	6.P.M.	600X new in GORDON LINE B Coy deepened + widened ABERDEEN LINE between FLEET S. C	
"	"		A + C Coys continued wiring of GORDON LINE.	

Army Form C. 2118.

WAR DIARY
or
INTELLIGENCE SUMMARY.

(Erase heading not required.)

Instructions regarding War Diaries and Intelligence Summaries are contained in F. S. Regs., Part II. and the Staff Manual respectively. Title pages will be prepared in manuscript.

Place	Date	Hour	Summary of Events and Information	Remarks and references to Appendices
CHOCQUES MAREOUET	29.6.18	6 P.M.	A & C Coys continued wiring GORDON LINE. B Coy erected 6x3 wire BLACK LINE & completed ABERDEEN TRENCH to standard dimensions except actual water protection the full depth being attained by completion wiring of "BLACK LINE" - C. Coy continued to completed wiring of	
"	30.6.18	6 P.M.	A & B Coys continued work (wiring) of standard pattern ie - 3 feet double apron fence - GORDON LINE to standard pattern.	

A. D. Cotter
Major.
Comdg. 26th K. R. R. Corps

20th. (S) BATTALION KINGS ROYAL RIFLE CORPS. (PIONEERS).

SECRET.

OPERATION ORDER No. 2.

Reference 1/10,000 Sheet 36A. S.E. 4 (LOCON).

1. (a) On the night 13th./14th. June a readjustment of Brigade Fronts will take place, and the Divisional Front will be held with 3 Brigades in the Line.
   (b) On completion of readjustment, Brigades will be disposed as follows:-

   <u>8th. Inf. Brigade (right)</u>

   Brigade H.Q. - Canal Bank in W.2.c.

   <u>9th. Inf. Brigade (centre).</u>

   Brigade H.Q. - E.4.b.4.1.

   <u>76th. Inf. Brigade (left).</u>

   Brigade H.Q. - L'ABBAYE.

   Boundaries between Brigades are shown on attached Map (O.C. Coys. only).

2. With a view to securing a greater depth in defence on the East Bank of the LA BASSEE Canal, the 3rd. Division will advance its front on the night 14th./15th. June to the line - Q.34.d.4.2. FORD LANE - TURBEAUTE O.T. at W.12.a.0.8 - thence along the West bank of this stream to W.12.c.1.6 - thence to W.12.b.5.8 where it will connect up with our present front line.
   (b) The 4th. Division has been ordered to conform by advancing their extreme right flank to gain touch with the left flank of the 3rd. Division about Q.34.d.40.25.
   (c) The operation will be carried out as a surprise without a preliminary bombardment.

3. The operation will be carried out by one Battalion of the 9th. Inf. Brigade (4th. Royal Fusiliers), plus 2 Platoons of 1st. Northumberland Fusiliers on the right, and two Battalions of the 76th. Inf. Brigade (2nd. Suffolks and 1st. Gordon Highlanders) on the left. The 8th. Inf. Brigade will advance its left to conform to the forward movement of the 9th. Inf. Brigade. One Coy. of 1st. Royal Scots Fusiliers will be used for this purpose.
   The dividing line between the 9th. and 76th. Inf. Brigades will be the road running N.E. from W.11.b.0.5.
   ZERO hour will be communicated later.

4. (a) On the night 15th./16th. June the work of wiring the line of resistance (i.e., present outpost lines), will be commenced by the Battalion. Coys. have been allotted as under for this work :-

   (b) <u>76th. Inf. Brigade Sector.</u>   "A" Coy. plus 2 Platoons of "C" Coy.

   (a) <u>9th. Inf. Brigade Sector.</u>   "B" Coy. plus 2 Platoons of "C" Coy.

   (c) <u>Tasks for night 15th./16th. June.</u>

   "A" Coy. and 2 Platoons of "C" Coy. will erect one Belt of fence and double apron wire from FLEET STREET W.11.b.2.8 to PARK LANE

2.

W.4.d.7.9. – distance 1000 yds.
This Belt will be erected 50 yds. to 60 yds. from trench line.

(d) "B" Coy. and 2 Platoons of "C" Coy. will erect 1 Belt of fence and double apron wire from end of wire erected by "C" Coy. at W.17.b.95.45 along the "line of resistance" to connect up with "A" Coy. at FLEET STREET W.11.b.2.3. – distance about 1000 yds.
This Belt will be 50 yds. to 60 yds. from trench line.

(e) Tasks for night 16th./17th. June. "A" Coy. and 2 Platoons of "C" Coy. will erect a Belt of fence and double apron between the Belt erected on night 15th./16th. and the trench. Inner edge to be 25 yds. to 35 yds. from trench line.

(f) "B" Coy. and 2 Platoons of "C" Coy. will erect a Belt of fence and double apron between the Belt erected on night 15th./16th. and the trench. Inner edge to be 25 yds. to 35 yds. from trench line.

5. DUMPS. 76th. Inf. Brigade.
(a) Dumps of wire and pickets have been made at the following points :-
W.4.d.4.5. : W.11.a.1.4.
W.11.a.4.7. : W.11.a.8.9.

A sufficient quantity of material for the 1st. nights work has already been got forward by 76th. Inf. Brigade to these DUMPS.
It is hoped to get enough for the two nights forward before the night 14th./15th. Material allotted for the 2 Belts :-
750 Long Screw Pickets.
1500 Medium " "
375 Coils Barbed Wire.

(b) 9th. Inf. Brigade.
The following materials have been dumped in wood at W.17.b.8.8 for the use of "B" Coy. and 2 Platoons of "C" Coy. :-
750 Long Angle Irons. Screw Pickets.
1500 Medium Screw Pickets.
375 Coils Barbed Wire.

6. BRIDGES. 76th. Inf. Brigade. Area.
(a) The Canal will be bridged at the following points :-

W.11.a.0.4.
W.4.c.3.4.

Additional floating bridges are being put over the Canal at approximately the following points :-

W.11.a.2.2.
W.10.b.5.8.

(b) 9th. Inf Brigade Area.
"B" Coy. will cross the LA BASSEE Canal at any of the bridges S. of BAS D'ANNEZIN.

7. MEDICAL ARRANGEMENTS. 76th. Inf. Brigade Area.
(a) Regimental Aid Posts will be established at :-
W.11.a.0.4 - 2nd. Suffolk Regt.
W.4.c.3.4. - 1st. Gordon Highlanders.
Walking wounded will be directed to Advanced Dressing Station at L'ABBAYE.
(b) 9th. Inf. Brigade Area. Regimental Aid Post will be established in PERTH LINE at W.18.c.1.5. (4th. R.F's) and at LA PLOUY FARM.

3.

Walking wounded will be directed to Advanced Dressing Station at ANNEZIN.

8. ACKNOWLEDGE.

J. F. Howell
Capt. & Adjutant.
The King's Royal Rifle Corps.
20th. (S) Bn. (Pioneers).

13th. June 1918.

Copies to :-

3rd. Division "G".
8th. Inf. Brigade.
9th. Inf. Brigade.
76th. Inf. Brigade.
C.R.E.
D.M.G.C.
O.C. "A" Coy.
O.C. "B" Coy.
O.C. "C" Coy.
O.C. Transport.
Commanding Officer.
WAR DIARY (2).
File.

Army Form C. 2118.

20 K.R.R.C.

WAR DIARY
or
INTELLIGENCE SUMMARY.
(Erase heading not required.)

Instructions regarding War Diaries and Intelligence Summaries are contained in F. S. Regs., Part II. and the Staff Manual respectively. Title pages will be prepared in manuscript.

Place	Date	Hour	Summary of Events and Information	Remarks and references to Appendices
CHOCQUES MAREQUET	1.7.18	6.P.M.	"A" Coy erected 600 yards good road at PONT HINGES. B. Coy erected 600 yards on front of BLACK LINE on the right by CANAL LANE in Three delderates 250 yards wire in W. 24. a. This completes three lefts of wire from LA BASSEE CANAL to the start at DE LA LAVIE. "C" Coy erected 450 of wire erected in this left in front of new French position N.E. from retient W. 2o. F. 75. from PERTH TRENCH.	
"	2.7.18	6.P.M.	A. Coy erected 400 yards around Strongpoint at W.10.V.V.91. B Coy commenced erecting SPIDER wire entanglement between Hiding Hills of mines on GORDON LINE. C Coy continued wiring of PERTH SWITCH - 500 yds erected.	
"	3.7.18	6 P.M.	A.Coy commenced wiring round Brotherhead at W.10.6.8.5. 400 erected. "B" Coy continued felling in Hiding wing on GORDON LINE with SPIDER web entanglement. C. Coy continued wiring of PERTH (SWITCH 600 erected.	
"	4.7.18	6pm	work continued as for 3.7.18.	
"	5.7.18	6pm	A Coy completed bridge head at W.10.6.6.6. B Coy (2 platoons) SPIDER web entanglement on GORDON LINE. C. Coy started Spider web entanglement on PERTH LINE. Starting at LAVIE CANAL.	
"	6.7.18	6pm	Commenced wiring bridge head at W. 11. a. 3. 1. - C & B. Coy continued wiring GORDON & PERTH.	
"	7.7.18	6pm	All days continued wiring as for 6.7.18. Continual shelling hindered work.	
"	8.7.18	6pm	A Coy dug 300× barbed wire below from ABERDEEN LINE & LOCON. B Coy dug 300× barbed. French army supplied posts in GLASGOW SWITCH. C. Coy formed supply dump of posts in GLASGOW LINE.	
"	9.7.18	6pm	A B & C Coys demolished work on ABERDEEN LINE from division line at M.B.5.0.	
"	10.7.18	6pm	A & B. Coys continued work on ABERDEEN LINE. C. Coy, 1 platoon on agricultural work & 3 plats on Jordan concrete MG posts	
"	11.7.18	6pm	A.B + C Coys continued work as for 10.7.18.	
"	12.7.18	6pm	continued work as for 11.7.18	
"	13.7.18	6pm	A Coy erected 300× cross spider web entanglement on PERTH LINE - B Coy erected 75× spider web on GORDON LINE - A Coy completed work as for M.B.5.0.	
"	14.7.18	6pm	All Coys continued work as for 13 inst.	
"	15.7.18	6pm	Continued as for 14th inst.	
"	16.7.18	6pm	Con. (Francis) as for 15 inst.	

WAR DIARY
or
INTELLIGENCE SUMMARY.
(Erase heading not required.)

Army Form C. 2118.

Instructions regarding War Diaries and Intelligence Summaries are contained in F. S. Regs., Part II. and the Staff Manual respectively. Title pages will be prepared in manuscript.

Place	Date	Hour	Summary of Events and Information	Remarks and references to Appendices
CHOQUES MAREQUET	17.7.18	6 p.m.	A + B Coys det. 365 x forward posts from GORDON LINE at W.10.d.3.3. to FLEET ST. C Coy continued as before —	
—	18.7.18	6 p.m.	A + B Coys det. 360 x forward posts from FLEET ST to GORDON LINE at W.16.b.8.5 — C Coy rel'd 18thD	
—	19.7.18	6 p.m.	A + B Coys relieved 50th Div on nightwork in GORDON LINE. C Coy continued worksparty. 1 Platoon 3a A + 3	
—	20.7.18	6 p.m.	A Coy two platoons + B Coy continued working parties — 1 Platoon 3a A + C	
—	21.7.18	6 p.m.	Worked on L/G valley at HINGES —	
—	22.7.18	6 p.m.	Continued work as p.m. 20 & 21 inst.	
—	23.7.18	6 p.m.	A Coy two platoons + B Coy working GORDON LINE — 1 Platoon A + A Coy at mass dump at LASSIGNEE	
—	24.7.18	6 p.m.	B + 2 platoons C Coy working mass employment to PERT H LINE —	
—	25.7.18	6 p.m.	A & C Coys mass employment to GORDON + PERT H LINES —	
—	26.7.18	6 p.m.	Continued work at p.m. 24.7.18	
—	27.7.18	6 p.m.	Continued work about GORDON + PERTH LINES —	
—	28.7.18	6 p.m.	Continued work as p.m. 26.7.18	
—	29.7.18	6 p.m.	A B + C Coys continued employment to PERTH LINE	
—	30.7.18	6 p.m.	A Coy rested & out on nightwork on Burlde post in ABERDEEN LINE & W.L.B.I.3 - B + A Coys continued mass employment to GORDON LINE —	
—	31.7.18	6 p.m.	A Coy continued work on post in ABERDEEN LINE — B Coy continued employment post on GORDON LINE — C Coy continued work in GORDON LINE —	

Russell Martin Lt Col
Comdg 4th KRRC

Army Form C. 2118.

20th K.R.R.C.

WAR DIARY
or
INTELLIGENCE SUMMARY.

(Erase heading not required.)

Instructions regarding War Diaries and Intelligence Summaries are contained in F.S. Regs., Part II. and the Staff Manual respectively. Title pages will be prepared in manuscript.

Place	Date	Hour	Summary of Events and Information	Remarks and references to Appendices
CHOCQUES.	1.8.18	6pm	Battalion working on EVIN BURGH lines at W.H.4.B.1.5. and on GORDON LINE revetting & widening French	
MAREQUET.	2.8.18	6pm	work on ABERDEEN LINE & GORDON LINE, putting in trench boards & revetting -	
	3.8.18	6pm	Continued work as for 2.8.18.	
	4.8.18	6pm	Continued work as for 3.8.18.	
	5.8.18	6pm	Continued work as for 4.8.18.	
	6.8.18		do	
BURBURE	7.8.18	12pm	Moved Battalion to BURBURE - move completed by 11.30 am -	
	8.8.18	6pm	Battalion Training.	
PRESSY LES	9.8.18	6pm	Travel to PRESSY arriving at 11.45 am. Every coy. commanded by junior Battalion at 2.35 pm.	
PERNES	10.8.18	6pm	Battalion Training -	
	11.8.18	12pm	(CHURCH PARADE)	
	12.8.18	6pm	Battalion Training - Corps Horse show -	
GROUCHES	13.8.18	6pm	Battalion moved by train to GROUCHES. Transport by road).	
	14.8.18	6pm	Battalion Training.	
	15.8.18	6pm	Battalion Training - Transport arrived at 4 am -	
	16.8.18	6pm	Battalion Training -	
	17.8.18	6pm	Battalion Training -	
	18.8.18	12pm	do.	
	19.8.18	6pm	CHURCH PARADE - Sports in afternoon -	
BIENVILLERS	20.8.18	6pm	Training - Sports in afternoon.	
PURPLE RESERVE	21.8.18	6pm	Moved from GROUCHES at 10.30 pm on 19.8.18. marched to BIENVILLERS, arriving at 5 am -	
	22.8.18	6pm	Division attacked & took line of Railway.	
	23.8.18	6pm	Night 23rd worked on tracks in forward area -	
	24.8.18	6pm	Continued work on tracks. Moved to trenches at COURCELLES.	
PURPLE LINE.	25.8.18	6pm	Advanced via COURCELLES - ERVILLERS - moved into front PURPLE LINE as CORPS RESERVE -	
	26.8.18	6pm	do.	
	27.8.18	6pm	Working on roads. AYETTE - MOYENNEVILLE -	
MOYENNEVILLE	28.8.18	6pm	Moved to MOYENNEVILLE -	
	29.8.18	6pm	Work on MAMBLAINCOURT- ERVILLERS Rd	
	30.8.18	6pm	Work on ERVILLERS - ST LEGER Rd	
	31.8.18	6pm	Work on ST LEGER - CROISILLES Rd	

Intelligence Officer
20th K.R.R.C.

20th N.R.R.P.C. **WAR DIARY** or **INTELLIGENCE SUMMARY**

Army Form C. 2118.

Place	Date	Hour	Summary of Events and Information	Remarks and references to Appendices
MOYENNEVILLE	1.9.18	6.pm	Finished off ERVILLERS - ST LEGER - CROISILLES Road.	
ST LEGER (BANK TRENCH)	2.9.18	6.pm	Moved to BANK TRENCH - commenced work on MORY - ECOUST Road.	
"	3.9.18	6.pm	Work on ECOUST - NOREUIL Road + ECOUST - MORY road.	
"	4.9.18	6.pm	Work on ECOUST - NOREUIL - LAGNICOURT Roads.	
"	5.9.18	6.pm	Work on ECOUST - NOREUIL - LAGNICOURT Roads.	
"	6.9.18	6.pm	Moved to BIENVILLERS at rest.	
BIENVILLERS	7.9.18	6.pm	Rested.	
"	8.9.18	6.pm	Rested.	
"	9.9.18	6.pm	Training - harassed by rain. Bn. placed under orders of C.E. Corps - recd orders to move to BEAUMETZ area.	
COURCELLES	10.9.18	6.pm	Left BIENVILLERS at 10 a.m. arrived at COURCELLES 5 p.m. - Heavy rains made marching very difficult.	
Bucquoy Shed I.23.a.7.7	11.9.18	6.pm	Left COURCELLES at 10 a.m. arrived at I.23.a.7.7. 4.30 p.m.	
"	12.9.18	6.pm	Work on BEUMETZ - DOIGNIES - HERMIES road.	
"	13.9.18	6.pm	Work on BEUMETZ - DOIGNIES - HERMIES road. One Co. (c) working on roller of railway	
"	14.9.18	6.pm	Construction Co. on BEUMETZ - RAMP on CANAL DU NORD.	
"	15.9.18	6.pm	Work on BEUMETZ - DOIGNIES - HERMIES road - "C" Co working on RAMP.	
"	16.9.18	6.pm	Work on BEUMETZ - DOIGNIES - HERMIES road - "C" Co. working on RAMP.	
"	17.9.18	6.pm	Work on BEUMETZ - DOIGNIES - HERMIES - CANAL (K.J1.a.0.3) Road - "C" Co. working on RAMP.	
"	18.9.18	6.pm	Work on BEUMETZ - DOIGNIES - HERMIES - CANAL (K.31.a.0.3) Road - "C" Co. working on RAMP.	
"	19.9.18	6.pm	Work on BEUMETZ - DOIGNIES - HERMIES - CANAL Road - "B" Co. BEUMETZ - HERMIES Rd -	
"	20.9.18	6.pm	"A" Co. working on DOIGNIES - CANAL RAMP Road - "B" Co. on BEUMETZ - HERMIES Rd. -	
"	21.9.18	6.pm	"C" Co. on YORKSHIRE BANK Rd. - "C" Co. working on YORKSHIRE BANK Rd. -	
"	22.9.18	6.pm	A + B Cos on BEUMETZ - HERMIES BANK Rd. -	
"	23.9.18	6.pm	A + C Cos working on YORKSHIRE BANK Rd. -	

Army Form C. 2118.

WAR DIARY
or
INTELLIGENCE SUMMARY.
(Erase heading not required.)

Instructions regarding War Diaries and Intelligence Summaries are contained in F. S. Regs., Part II. and the Staff Manual respectively. Title pages will be prepared in manuscript.

Place	Date	Hour	Summary of Events and Information	Remarks and references to Appendices
I.23.a.7.7.	24.9.18	6pm	A & C Coys continued work on YORKSHIRE BANK Rd - mashing foundation & laying slabs on it - (continued) work on CANAL BANK at K.20.6.5.8.	B Coy.
HERMES	25.9.18	6pm	Head quarters & rear co. moved to HERMES. Coys continued work as for 24.9.18.	
"	26.9.18	6pm	Company continued work as for 25/9/18.	
"	27.9.18	6pm	"	
"	28.9.18	6pm	Shell holes filled in shell holes FLESQUIERES - HAVRINCOURT - RIBECOURT roads.	
"	29.9.18	6pm	All coys continued work on roads as for 28.9.18 -	
FLESQUIERES	30.9.18	6pm	Battalion moved to huts near FLESQUIERES - work continued on roads -	

Lieut Col. Montrougy
Comdg. XX K.R.R.C.

A.5834 Wt. W4973/M687 750,000 8/16 D. D. & L. Ltd. Forms/C.2118/13.

20 K.R.R.C.

R/3

Vol 28

WAR DIARY or INTELLIGENCE SUMMARY

Army Form C. 2118.

(Erase heading not required.)

Place	Date	Hour	Summary of Events and Information	Remarks and references to Appendices
RIBECOURT	1.10.18	6pm	Battalion moved to RIBECOURT — move completed by 10.30 a.m.	
"	2.10.18	"	Refitted, kit insp. & shower bath. MARCOING — MASNIERES	
"	3.10.18	"	All companys continued work on MARCOING — CAMBRAI & MARCOING — MASNIERES Roads	
"	4.10.18	"	work continued as p.m. 3rd MASNIERES VILLAGE Shelled also road to RUMILLY	
"	5.10.18	"	Continued work on roads as for 4th special attention being paid to draining	
"	6.10.18	"	"	
"	7.10.18	"		
"	8.10.18	"	Whid in Wakefield huts on E side of towing path CANAL DE ST QUENTIN moved dug out the heel on N side of MARCOING MASNIERES Rd 4 forward dug outs self on tow path on ST QUENTIN	
"			CAMBRAI Rd	
"	9.10.18	6pm	worked on roads through MASNIERES to CREVECOURT, also repairing dug outs on track from	
"			MARCOING — MASNIERES.	
"	10.10.18	"	Continued work as for 9th inst.	
"	11.10.18	"	Continued work on MARCOING — CREVECOURT and RUMILLY Roads	
"	12.10.18	"	Battalion moved to CREVECOURT area	
CREVECOURT	13.10.18	6pm	A Coy worked on CREVECOURT — SERENVILLERS road. B Coy CREVECOURT — RUMILLY Rd	
"	14.10.18	"	C Coy. CREVECOURT — CAMBRAI road	
"	15.10.18	"	Continued work on same	
"	16.10.18	"		
"	17.10.18	"		
"	18.10.18	"	MASNIERES — CREVECOURT and RUMILLY Roads	
"	19.10.18	"	Battalion moved to QUIEVY arriving at 3.30 p.m.	
QUIEVY	20.10.18	"	worked on QUIEVY — SOLESMES Rd	
"	21.10.18	"	Continued work on QUIEVY — SOLESMES Rd	
"	22.10.18	"		
"	23.10.18	"	Battalion moved to SOLESMES arriving at 11.30 a.m. 4 Coy(s) on SOLESMES — ROMERIES	
SOLESMES	24.10.18	"		

WAR DIARY
or
INTELLIGENCE SUMMARY.

(Erase heading not required.)

Army Form C. 2118.

Place	Date	Hour	Summary of Events and Information	Remarks and references to Appendices
SOLESMES	25.10.18	6pm	Worked on SOLESMES ROMERIES BEAUDIGNIES sect: of LOMMEL - VERTAIN Rly	
"	26.10.18	6pm	Reorganised work as for 25th unit	
"	27.10.18	6pm	Continued work as on 26th unit	
"	28.10.18	6pm	A Coy worked on TROUSEE MINON - ESCARMAIN rd - B Coy ROMERIES - BEAUDIGNIES Rd. C Coy located on route to ESCARMAIN	
"	29.10.18	6pm	Continued work as for 28th unit	
"	30.10.18	6pm	— 29th "	
"	31.10.18	9pm	— 30th "	

Cloadwell-Martin
Lieut Col
Comdg 253 Army Troops Coy RE

201 W.R.R.C
(riounts)

Army Form C. 2118.

WAR DIARY
or
INTELLIGENCE SUMMARY.
(Erase heading not required.)

Instructions regarding War Diaries and Intelligence Summaries are contained in F. S. Regs., Part II. and the Staff Manual respectively. Title pages will be prepared in manuscript.

Place	Date	Hour	Summary of Events and Information	Remarks and references to Appendices
SOLESMES	1.11.18	5 am	Bn moved to LE QUESNOY BLANC – VERTAIN Rd and SOLESMES – ROMERIES Rd. diag G	
	2.11.18			
	3.11.18		BELLEVUE Fm Rd	
	4.11.18		RUESNES – LE QUESNOY road & RUESNES – BELLEVUE FM Rd	
RUESNES	5.11.18		Battalion moved to RUESNES arriving at 12.50	
"	6.11.18	6 pm	Battalion moved to LE QUESNOY – BAVAI Rd mostly at sites with (trees) also in the sunk plain	
"	7.11.18	4 pm	3.515 with buckle + medal	
"	8.11.18	4 pm		
"	9.11.18	4 pm	Armistice signed hostilities ceased at 11 am – week commencing on LE QUESNOY – BAVAI Rd	
"	10.11.18	4 pm		
"	11.11.18	4 pm	Battalion moved to	
"	12.11.18	4 pm	Battalion moved to	
BOMMEGNIES	13.11.18	4 pm	BOMMEGNIES arr arriving at 13.15 – March to Germany commences	
NEUFMESNIL	14.11.18	4 pm	Neuf Mesnil arriving at 19.00 hours	
LOUVROIL	15.11.18	4 pm	Louvroil arriving at 14.50 hours	
COUSOLRE	16.11.18	4 pm	Cousolre arriving at 13.50 hours	
"	17.11.18	4 pm	Battalion marked to	
	18.11.18	4 pm	Bousignies Road clearing up repairing	
	19.11.18	4 pm	BERSILLIES L'ABBAYE Rd	
THUIN	20.11.18	4 pm	2nd Spots in char church parade at 10am Thanksgiving services	
MALINNES	21.11.18	4 pm	Battalion moved to THUIN arriving at 13.30 hours	
BIESMES	22.11.18	4 pm	MALINNES arriving at 14.15 hours	
ROUILLON	23.11.18	4 pm	BIESMES – 12.30 hours	
NATOYE	24.11.18	4 pm	ROUILLON – 14.30 hours	
PESSOUX	25.11.18	4 pm	NATOYE – 14.15 hours very hard march road heavy + very hilly	
	26.11.18	4 pm	PESSOUX – 11.30	
	27.11.18		Rested at PESSOUX	

R Russell Mackenzie
Lt XX K.R.R.C

A6834 Wt. W4973/M687 750,000 8/16 D. D. & L. Ltd. Forms/C.2118/13.

On His Majesty's Service.

20th K.R.R.C. (PIONEERS)

DECEMBER 1918.

WAR DIARY or INTELLIGENCE SUMMARY

Army Form C. 2118.

20 KRR / V030

Place	Date	Hour	Summary of Events and Information	Remarks and references to Appendices
PESSOUX	1.12.18	6pm	All Coys rested, cleaned	
	2.12.18	6pm	Motor lorry drill, physical training, afternoon recreation	
	3.12.18	6pm		
BAILLONVILLE	4.12.18	6pm	Battalion moved to BAILLONVILLE arriving at 1pm	
MELREUX	5.12.19	6pm	Battalion paraded at 7.45am (marched at head of Brigade) to MELREUX arriving at 12.00	
MORMONT	6.12.19	6pm	paraded at 08.00 (marched) to MORMONT arriving at 13.00. Very bad billets	
MALEMPRÉ	7.12.18	6pm	Battalion paraded at 08.15 (marched) to MALEMPRÉ arriving at 11.30 –	
SART	8.12.19	6pm	Battalion (marched) off at 09.00, arrived at SART at 13.30. A Coy billeted in SART (B Coy at COMTE B Coy at JOUBIEVAL – Village very small, great difficulty in Meir billets for all the men –	
BOVIGNY	9.12.18	6pm	Battalion paraded at 08.30 hours (marched) to BOVIGNY arriving at 12.15, very irregular & disjointed up –	
BOVIGNY	10.12.18	6pm	Rested & cleaned up –	
THOMMEN (GERMANY)	11.12.18	6pm	Battalion moved off at 08.15 and crossed the German frontier at 10.30 hours – the Coys (Commanded took the salute) the Bugles playing the Regimental March. All the men had food billets. Weather above brites.	
HEUEM	12.12.18	6pm	Marched to HEUEM arriving at 13.60. Very heavy marching, roads paved through ST.VITH –	
HALLSCHLAG	13.12.18	6pm	Marched to HALLSCHLAG arriving at 13.80. Very heavy marching, very hilly, road distance 14 miles. The men stood the march well.	
SCHMIDTHEIM	14.12.18	6pm	Moved off at 09.15 arrived at SCHMIDTHEIM at 13.15 – very wet –	
SCHONAU	15.12.18	6pm	Marched to SCHONAU arriving at 14.15, a long march –	
KIRSPENICH	16.12.18	6pm	Marched to KIRSPENICH arriving at 12.50, easy march, men very tired –	
EUSKIRCHEN	17.12.18	6pm	Moved to EUSKIRCHEN arriving at 11.30 – men have good billets – (pass through MUNSTEREIFEL)	

Army Form C. 2118.

WAR DIARY
or
INTELLIGENCE SUMMARY.
(Erase heading not required.)

Instructions regarding War Diaries and Intelligence Summaries are contained in F. S. Regs., Part II. and the Staff Manual respectively. Title pages will be prepared in manuscript.

Place	Date	Hour	Summary of Events and Information	Remarks and references to Appendices
FUSSENICH	18.12.18	6pm	Battalion marches to FUSSENICH arriving at 12.15 hours	
DUREN	19.12.18	6pm	Battalion marches to DUREN & billeted in disused factory & barracks on arrival	
	20.12.18	1pm	Moved into Black C. & F	
	21.12.18 to 31.12.18	6pm	Remained training & recreation	
		6pm	Continued training & recreation	

Russell Martin Lt Col
Comg. x x KRRC.

Instructions regarding War Diaries and Intelligence Summaries are contained in F. S. Regs., Part II. and the Staff Manual respectively. Title pages will be prepared in manuscript.

WAR DIARY
or
INTELLIGENCE SUMMARY.
(Erase heading not required.)

Army Form C. 2118.

Place	Date	Hour	Summary of Events and Information	Remarks and references to Appendices
[illegible]	[illegible]	[illegible]	[illegible] cleaning [illegible]	
[illegible]	[illegible]	[illegible]	[illegible] … [illegible]	
…LLON[VILLE]	[illegible]	[illegible]	Battalion moved to BAILLONVILLE arriving at 1 pm —	
…REUX	5.12.18	[illegible]	Battalion paraded at 7.45 am marched at head of Brigade to MELREUX arriving at 12.00	
…RMONT	6.12.18	[illegible]	Paraded at 08.00 & marched to MORMONT arriving at 13.00 very bad billets —	
…LEMPRE	7.12.18	[illegible]	Battalion paraded at 08.15 marched to MALEMPRÉ arriving at 11.30 —	
…RT.	8.12.18	[illegible]	Battalion marched off at 09.00 & arrived at SART at 13.30. HQ & [illegible] billeted in SART	
			[illegible] Coy at COMTE [illegible] Coy at JOUBIEVAL — villages very small great difficulty	
			in obtaining billets for all the men —	
…VIGNY	9.12.18	[illegible]	Battalion paraded at 08.30 hours marched to BOVIGNY arriving at 12.15, easy	
			march & better billets.	
…IGNY	10.12.18	[illegible]	Rested & cleaned up —	
…MMEN (…MANY)	11.12.18	[illegible]	Battalion moved off at 08.15 and crossed the German frontier at 10.30 hours. The	
			Corps Commander taking the salute, the bugles playing the regimental march.	
			All the men had good billets & rations were better —	
…UEM.	12.12.18	[illegible]	marched to HEUEM arriving at 13.00 very heavy marching passed through ST. VITH.	
…SCHLAG	13.12.18	[illegible]	marched to HALLSCHLAG arriving at 13.30 very heavy marching, very hilly,	
			[illegible] hard distance [illegible] miles, the men stuck the march well —	
…DTHEIM	14.12.18	[illegible]	moved off at 09.15 arrived at SCHMIDTHEIM at 13.15. very wet —	
…NAU	[illegible]	[illegible]	marched to SCHONAU arriving at 14.15 a long march [illegible] hilly —	
…FENICH	[illegible]	[illegible]	marched to KIRSPENICH arriving at 13.00 easy march passed through MUNSTEREIFEL	
…CHEN	[illegible]	[illegible]	[illegible] to EUSKIRCHEN arrived at 11.30 [illegible] good billets —	

Army Form C. 2118.

WAR DIARY
or
INTELLIGENCE SUMMARY.
(Erase heading not required.)

Place	Date	Hour	Summary of Events and Information	Remarks and references to Appendices
FUSSENICH				
DÜREN				

**3RD DIVISION
DIVL. TROOPS**

20TH (S) BATTALION
K.R.R.C. (PIONEERS)
JAN-DEC 1917.

20th (S) Battn. King's Royal Rifle Corps (Pioneers)

Vol 8/10

War Diary

for

January 1st 1917 to January 31st 1917

Volume X

Army Form C. 2118.

WAR DIARY
or
INTELLIGENCE SUMMARY.
(Erase heading not required.)

Place	Date	Hour	Summary of Events and Information	Remarks and references to Appendices
Courcelles	1/1/17	6p.m.	A.B.C. Coys. continued work on C.T.'s in the Arruvual Area. D Coy continued work on dug-outs. Coy. tramways, and on R.E. dump for 56th Field Coy. R.E.'s	
Courcelles	2/1/17	6p.m.	A.B.C. Coys. carried on with work on C.T.'s. D Coy carried on with work for 56th Field Coy.	
Courcelles	3/1/17	6p.m.	A.B.C. Coys continued working on main C.T.'s. D Coy continued with usual work for 56th Field Coy.	
Courcelles	4/1/17	6p.m.	A.B.C. Coys continued working on main C.T.'s. D Coy carried on with work for 56th Field Coy. R.E.'s.	
Courcelles	5/1/17	6p.m.	A.B.C. Coys. carried on with work on main C.T.'s. D Coy carried on with usual work for 57th Field Coy. R.E.'s	
Courcelles	6/1/17	6p.m.	All Companies were distributed as for 5th inst. and carried on same work.	

Army Form C. 2118.

WAR DIARY
or
INTELLIGENCE SUMMARY

(Erase heading not required.)

Instructions regarding War Diaries and Intelligence Summaries are contained in F. S. Regs., Part II. and the Staff Manual respectively. Title Pages will be prepared in manuscript.

Place	Date	Hour	Summary of Events and Information	Remarks and references to Appendices
Courcelles	7/1/17	6 p.m	B Coy and ½ C Coy. worked on the clearance of Railway Avenue. 1 Platoon of D Coy. continued work to complete the remainder of the 13 Bttn. prepared for move.	
Montrelet	8/1/17	12 n.n	The Battn. moved from Courcelles to Huntrelet. They marched to Puro and were conveyed by motor lorries from Puro to Huntrelet; movement being completed by 12 n.n.	
Candas	9/1/17	6 p.m.	The Battalion moved from Montrelet to Candas. 2 Coys. and ½ Coy. were billeted in Candas in Zenneglise. "C" Coy commenced work on R.E. Dumps at Candas.	
Candas	10/1/17	6 p.m.	All available men were sent out to work on R.E. Dumps and G.H.Q. Ammunition Dumps in the vicinity of Candas.	
Candas	11/1/17	6 p.m.	Same work continued by all available men.	
Candas	12/1/17	6 p.m.	The Battalion continued work on R.E and Ammunition Dumps.	
Candas	13/1/17	6 p.m	Work as for 12th inst.	
Candas	14/1/17	6 p.m	Work as for 13th inst.	
Candas	15/1/17	6 p.m	Work as for 14th inst	

Army Form C. 2118.

WAR DIARY
or
INTELLIGENCE SUMMARY

(Erase heading not required.)

Place	Date	Hour	Summary of Events and Information	Remarks and references to Appendices
Candas	16/4/17	6p.m	Work continued as for 15th inst.	
Candas	17/4/17	6p.m	Work continued as for 16th inst.	
Candas	18/4/17	6p.m	Work continued as for 17th inst.	
Candas	19/4/17	6p.m	Work continued as for 18th inst.	
Candas	20/4/17	6p.m	Work continued as for 19th inst.	
Candas	21/4/17	6p.m	Work continued as for 20th inst.	
Candas	22/4/17	6p.m	Work continued as for 21st inst.	
Candas	23/4/17	6p.m	Work continued as for 22nd inst.	
Candas	24/4/17	6p.m	Work continued as for 23rd inst.	
Candas	25/4/17	6p.m	Work continued as for 24th inst.	
Candas	26/4/17	6p.m	Work continued as for 25th inst.	
Candas	27/4/17	6p.m	Work continued as for 26th inst. until 12.0 noon when working parties were relieved by 31st Division preparatory to move into new area.	

Army Form C. 2118.

WAR DIARY
or
INTELLIGENCE SUMMARY.
(Erase heading not required.)

Instructions regarding War Diaries and Intelligence Summaries are contained in F. S. Regs., Part II. and the Staff Manual respectively. Title pages will be prepared in manuscript.

Place	Date	Hour	Summary of Events and Information	Remarks and references to Appendices
Santon	28/4/17	6pm	The Battalion marched from Santon to Bretow, arriving about 2 p.m.	
Haute Visé	29/4/17	6pm	The Battalion marched from Bretow to Haute Visé and Paravit, arriving about 3.30 p.m. A & B Coys were billeted at Paravit and H.Q., B.C. and W.B. at Haute Visé	
Ceuf	30/4/17	6pm	The Battalion marched from Haute Visé and Paravit to Ceuf, arriving about 5 p.m.	
Bailleul	31/4/17	6pm	The Battalion marched from Ceuf to Bailleul viâ Corbie. Vol. B. A and B Coys were billeted in Bailleul and C and D Coys in Maÿcourt.	
aux Cornailles			Cornailles and Maÿcourt-en-Corbie and Bailleul. All were settled in billets by 5.30 p.m.	R. Syfer Lieut C. 20 Comg

From O.C. 20th KRRC.
To Q. 3rd. Division.

<u>Secret</u>. Attached please find War Diary for the month of February 1917.

R. Dyke Lt Col
Comg. 20th KRRC.

Field.
1/3/17
R.I 24.

WAR DIARY
or
INTELLIGENCE SUMMARY.

(Erase heading not required.)

Army Form C. 2118.

20 K.R.R.C.

Place	Date	Hour	Summary of Events and Information	Remarks and references to Appendices
Ambrines	1/2/17	6 p.m.	The Battalion marched from Bailleul and Magnicourt to Ambrines arriving about 1 p.m.	
Ambrines	2/2/17	6 p.m.	The Battalion rested for the day in Ambrines.	
Arras	3/2/17	6 p.m.	Hd. Qs. and C and D Coys. marched to Arras arriving about 6.30 p.m. A and B Coys. remained in Ambrines to do work under C.E. 6th Corps.	
Arras	4/2/17	6 p.m.	'C' Coy. and half 'D' Coy. were engaged digging a new C.T. in front of the station Arras. A and B Coys. moved from Ambrines to Bel-les-Hameaux arriving about 1 p.m. They received orders to commence work on the 5th inst. constructing Armstrong huts and trenching the new C.T.	
Arras	5/2/17	6 p.m.	'C' Coy. and ½ 'D' Coy. commenced digging the new C.T. Inverness St. The other half 'D' Coy. commenced working on Dug-huts under the Lothian Field Coy R.E. A + B Coys. carried on with trenching at Bel. Es-Hameaux.	

Army Form C. 2118.

WAR DIARY
or
INTELLIGENCE SUMMARY.
(Erase heading not required.)

Instructions regarding War Diaries and Intelligence Summaries are contained in F. S. Regs., Part II. and the Staff Manual respectively. Title pages will be prepared in manuscript.

Place	Date	Hour	Summary of Events and Information	Remarks and references to Appendices
Arras	6/2/17	6p.m.	A and B Coys carried on with the bunking at Lyzl-les-Hameau. C and D Coys were distributed as for the 5th inst. 1½ Coys working on the new E.T. Havrencete St. and ½ Coy working on dug-outs with the Cheshire Field Coy R.E.	
Arras	7/2/17	6p.m.	The Coys carried on with same work as for the 6th inst.	
Arras	8/2/17	6p.m.	All work was continued as on the 7th inst.	
Arras	9/2/17	6p.m.	Work was continued as for the 8th inst.	
Arras	10/2/17	6p.m.	A and B Coys carried on with the bunking at Lyzl-les-Hameau. C Coy and half D Coy worked on the new sector of Imperial Innes; half D Coy continued work on Dug-outs with the Cheshire R.E.'s	
Arras	11/2/17	6p.m.	Work continued as for the 10th inst.	
Arras	12/2/17	6p.m.	Work continued as for the 11th inst.	
Arras	13/2/17	6p.m.	A, B, and half D Coy continued work as for the 12th inst. C and half D Coy started new sector of Twenty St.	
Arras	14/2/17	6p.m.	A and B Corps marched from Lyzl to Arras. They arrived about 7p.m. C and D Corps carried on as for the 13th inst.	

WAR DIARY
or
INTELLIGENCE SUMMARY.
(Erase heading not required.)

Army Form C. 2118.

Place	Date	Hour	Summary of Events and Information	Remarks and references to Appendices
Arras	15/9/17	6 p.m.	"A" and "B" Coy. rested. 3 Platoons of "C" Coy. and 2 Platoons of "D" Coy. carried on with new sector of Twenty St. One Platoon of "C" Coy. worked at cleaning and revetting the Eastern part of Imperial St. Two Platoons of "D" Coy. carried on with dug-outs with the Cheshire R.E's.	
Arras	16/9/17	6 p.m.	3 Platoons of "A" Coy and 3 Platoons of "B" Coy. carried on with new sector of Twenty St. 1 Platoon of "A" and 1 Platoon of "B" worked with Cheshire R.E's on dug-outs. 1 Platoon of "C" Coy worked on Imperial St and 1 Platoon of "D" on old sector of Twenty St. 3 Platoons of "C" and 3 Platoons of "D". Marched respectively to Liencourt and Wanquetin as a Hutting Detachment.	
Arras	17/9/17	6 p.m.	The Coys. were distributed as for 16th inst. and carried on with same work. The hutting parties commenced work.	O.L.

Army Form C. 2118.

WAR DIARY
or
INTELLIGENCE SUMMARY.
(Erase heading not required.)

Instructions regarding War Diaries and Intelligence Summaries are contained in F. S. Regs., Part II. and the Staff Manual respectively. Title pages will be prepared in manuscript.

Place	Date	Hour	Summary of Events and Information	Remarks and references to Appendices
Arras	18/9/17	6 p.m.	A and B Coy worked on shoring new sector of 15th from R.E. line to front line. The details of C Coy worked on clearing Imperial St. and the details of D Coy on clearing Twenty St. Wiring parties carried on with work at Lancourt and Wanquetin.	
Arras	19/9/17	6 p.m.	Platoon of A, 1 Platoon B, 1 details of D carried on works of clearing Twenty St. C Coy details were engaged on upkeep of Imperial St. Hutting parties as for 18th inst.	
Arras	20/9/17	6 p.m.	A Coy men working on Twenty St. B Coy in Jefter St. C Coy details on Imperial St and D Coy details on Leland St. Hutting parties as for 19th inst.	
Arras	21/9/17	6 p.m.	Same work was done as on for the 20th inst. with the exception that A Coy furnished a party to build Out Latrines and Rellable Blunders in the 3rd Div. Cecu.	
Arras	22/9/17	6 p.m.	As for the 21st inst with the exception that B Coy furnished a party to construct tracks into the woods into the Central CT.	
Arras	23/9/17	6 p.m.	All work as for 23rd inst	
Arras	24/9/17	6 p.m.	All work as for 24th inst	
Arras	25/9/17	6 p.m.	All work as for 25th inst	
Arras	26/9/17	6 p.m.	All work as for 25th inst	

Army Form C. 2118.

WAR DIARY
or
INTELLIGENCE SUMMARY.

(Erase heading not required.)

Instructions regarding War Diaries and Intelligence Summaries are contained in F.S. Regs., Part II. and the Staff Manual respectively. Title pages will be prepared in manuscript.

Place	Date	Hour	Summary of Events and Information	Remarks and references to Appendices
Arras	27/3/17	6 p.m.	All work was carried on as for the 26th inst.	
Arras	28/3/17	6 p.m.	All work as for the 27th inst.	

Leeds
28/3/17

R. Ryly Lt. M.
Comg. 2nd R.E.R.C.

Confidential

From O.C. 20th K.R.R.C.

To. 3rd Division G.

Herewith War Diary for the month of March please.

Field.
11/4/17

R. Myli
Comdg Lieut Colonel
20th K.R.R.C.

WAR DIARY
or
INTELLIGENCE SUMMARY.

(Erase heading not required.)

Army Form C. 2118.

20th KRRC Vol 9

Place	Date	Hour	Summary of Events and Information	Remarks and references to Appendices
Arras	1/3/17	6pm	3 Platoon of A Coy worked on Twenty St.; 1 Platoon of H on dept. Old Latrines in Cave. B 3 Platoon of B 3 Coy worked on Lyttleton St. and 1 Platoon on tunnels in Lateral C.T.) The details of C + D Coys were engaged on Imperial St. and Ireland St. respectively. The futting parties of C + D Coy carried on work at Lieucourt and Isanguetin respectively.	
Arras	2/3/17	6pm	All work was carried on as for the 1st inst.	
Arras	3/3/17	6pm	All work was carried on as for the 2nd inst.	
Arras	4/3/17	6pm	All work was carried on as for the 3rd inst, with the exception that a party of 16 men from "C" Coy were taken to Imperial St. and put on to opening up a new entrance to Quereus Cave.	
Arras	5/3/17	6pm	All work was carried on as for the 4th inst.	
Arras	6/3/17	6pm	All work was carried on as for the 5th inst.	
Arras	7/3/17	6pm	All work was carried on as for the 6th inst. A party reground the Ronfrancquels	
Arras	8/3/17	6pm	All work was carried on as for the 7th inst. yet except that a party from D Coy commenced work widening Tunnel (Crewe Tunnel)	
Arras	9/3/17	6pm	All work carried on as for the 8th	

Army Form C. 2118.

WAR DIARY
or
INTELLIGENCE SUMMARY.
(Erase heading not required.)

Instructions regarding War Diaries and Intelligence Summaries are contained in F. S. Regs., Part II. and the Staff Manual respectively. Title pages will be prepared in manuscript.

Place	Date	Hour	Summary of Events and Information	Remarks and references to Appendices
Arras	10/3/17	6pm	All work was carried on as for 9th inst except party commenced new entrance in Alladin Cave.	
Arras	11/3/17	6pm	All work was carried on as for 10th inst.	
Arras	12/3/17	6pm	All work was carried on as for 11th inst.	
Arras	13/3/17	6pm	All work was carried on as for 12th inst.	
Arras	14/3/17	6pm	All work was carried on as for 13th inst.	
Arras	15/3/17	6pm	All work was carried on as for 14th inst. except 1 platoon from A Coy and 1 Platoon from B Coy were distributed from work on Twenty S.T. and Fifteen S.T. Cee 2 and 2 ST. C.T. respectively and commenced work on Cee 2 and 2 ST. C.T. Inst.	
Arras	16/3/17	6pm	All work was carried on as for 15th inst.	
Arras	17/3/17	6pm	All work was carried on as for 16th except to the detachment of C Coy at Pierremont were moved to Wanquitin to work on Hutting, etc under charge water-ship.	
Arras	18/3/17	6pm	All work was carried on as for 17th inst.	
Arras	19/3/17	6pm	All work was carried on as for 18th except B Coy who were sent to dig an extension of C.T. from Fifteen St forward. Work was being carried out by R.E. and infantry. Any work done by Coy Commander, no work carried out	

C.L.

Army Form C. 2118.

WAR DIARY
or
INTELLIGENCE SUMMARY.
(Erase heading not required.)

Instructions regarding War Diaries and Intelligence Summaries are contained in F.S. Regs., Part II. and the Staff Manual respectively. Title pages will be prepared in manuscript.

Place	Date	Hour	Summary of Events and Information	Remarks and references to Appendices
Arras	20/3/17	6 p.m.	The Battalion was chiefly engaged on work on C.T's in the Divisional Area. Small parties worked on the latrines and ablution trenches in the Ronville Caves, and entrances to Rhadamés Cave, and the tunnels under the City. St Quentin Parade. 3rd party of 50 N.C.O.s & men returned from Arthur, Wanquetin.	
Arras	21/3/17	6 p.m.	Work was continued as for the 20th inst.	
Arras	22/3/17	6 p.m.	Work was continued as for the 21st inst.	
Arras	23/3/17	6 p.m.	Work was continued as for the 22nd inst, with the exception that 2 Platoons of 'A' Coy. were taken off C.T's and commenced building a road for Artillery from "Rue" Denfert, along 15th towards about G. 36. c. 9. 0.	
Arras	24/3/17	6 p.m.	Work was continued as for the 23rd inst. with the exception that 'B' Coy's party on the tunnels under the Rly. rd. Quartier Ronville were put on to C.T's having finished the tunnels.	
Arras	25/3/17	6 p.m.	Work was continued as for the 24th inst with the exception that 'A' Coy's party on the Artillery track went just in to C.T's, a party of Cavalry Pioneer being put on to work on Artillery track	
Arras	26/3/17	6 p.m.	Work was continued as for 25th inst	
Arras	27/3/17	6 p.m.	Work was continued as for 26th inst	2.

Army Form C. 2118.

WAR DIARY
or
INTELLIGENCE SUMMARY.
(Erase heading not required.)

Instructions regarding War Diaries and Intelligence Summaries are contained in F. S. Regs., Part II. and the Staff Manual respectively. Title pages will be prepared in manuscript.

Place	Date	Hour	Summary of Events and Information	Remarks and references to Appendices
Arran	28/3/17	6 p.m.	Work continued as for 27th inst with the exception that all Coys. had a small party preparing Forward Dumps for forthcoming operations	
Arran	29/3/17	6 p.m.	Work continued as for 28th inst.	
Arran	30/3/17	6 p.m.	Continued work on C.T.'s and preparation of Forward Dumps.	
Arran	31/3/17	6 p.m.	Continued work as for 30th inst	R.Lyle Lt.Col. Comg. 1. ? ????

From O.C. 20th KRRC
To 'Q' 3rd Division.

Enclosed please find War Diary for month of April.

R. Pyke Lt. Col.
Comg. 20th KRRC

Field
3/5/17

WAR DIARY
or
INTELLIGENCE SUMMARY.
(Erase heading not required.)

Army Form C. 2118.

20 KRR
J11/10

Place	Date	Hour	Summary of Events and Information	Remarks and references to Appendices
Arras	1/4/17	6p.m.	The whole Battalion were engaged in work in C.T's in the 3rd Divisional area with the exception of a small party per Company who were preparing forward Dumps before work in Cambrai Rd. in forthcoming operations.	
Arras	2/4/17	6p.m.	Continued work as for last week.	
Arras	3/4/17	6p.m.	Completed C.T's. 1 Coy. worked in northern Artillery track, and ½ Coy in fitting barricades in Cambrai Rd. ready to be removed on Y/Z night.	
Arras	4/4/17	6p.m.	Rested owing to Bombardment.	
Arras	5/4/17	6p.m.	As for 4th inst.	
Arras	6/4/17	6p.m.	3 Coys. rested 'D' Coy. filled in trenches and shell holes in Cambrai Rd. to our Front Line.	
Arras	7/4/17	6p.m.	3 Coy. rested, 'B' Coy. completed Cambrai Rd. to our Front Line	
Arras	8/4/17	6p.m.	3 Coy. rested, 'C' Coy. cleared Cambrai Rd. of barricades.	
Arras	9/4/17	10p.m.	The Battalion less 1½ Platoons completed a track for lorries in Cambrai Rd. from old German Front Line to tel Aumiral Corner. 1½ Platoon made Artillery track in order to get guns to South of Tilloy.	C.1

WAR DIARY
or
INTELLIGENCE SUMMARY.

(Erase heading not required.)

Army Form C. 2118.

Instructions regarding War Diaries and Intelligence Summaries are contained in F.S. Regs., Part II. and the Staff Manual respectively. Title pages will be prepared in manuscript.

Place	Date	Hour	Summary of Events and Information	Remarks and references to Appendices
Arras	10/4/17	6 p.m.	3½ Coy. continued works on Eastment Corner; wiring was made good by heavy traffic full width of road. ½ Coy. continued work on Artillery Track, Bortenzuging at Sant places.	
Arras	11/4/17	6 p.m.	Work was continued on Cambrai Rd. and Artillery Track.	
Arras	12/4/17	6 p.m.	Work was continued on Cambrai Rd. as far as Bois du Boeuf. The same party carried on with work on Artillery Track.	
Arras	13/4/17	6 p.m.	The whole Battalion worked for 8 hrs. on Cambrai Rd. from Rue du Temple to Bois du Boeuf.	
Arras	14/4/17	6 p.m.	Work was continued as for 13th inst.	
Arras	15/4/17	6 p.m.	Work was continued as for 14th inst.	
Arras	16/4/17	6 p.m.	Work was continued as for 15th inst.	
Arras	17/4/17	6 p.m.	Work was continued as for 16th inst.	
Arras	18/4/17	6 p.m.	Work was continued as for 17th inst.	
Arras	19/4/17	6 p.m.	Work was continued as for 18th inst.	
Arras	20/4/17	6 p.m.	Work was continued as for 19th inst.	

Army Form C. 2118.

WAR DIARY
or
INTELLIGENCE SUMMARY.
(Erase heading not required.)

Instructions regarding War Diaries and Intelligence Summaries are contained in F.S. Regs., Part II. and the Staff Manual respectively. Title pages will be prepared in manuscript.

Place	Date	Hour	Summary of Events and Information	Remarks and references to Appendices
Arras	21/4/17	6 p.m.	Work was continued on the Cambrai Rd.	
Arras	22/4/17	6 p.m.	Work was continued on for 21st inst.	
Arras	23/4/17	6 p.m.	The Battalion rested preparatory to moving forward.	
Arras & Tilloy	24/4/17	6 p.m.	The Battalion moved forward into sections allotted on following. A.B.C Coys. for work with the 76th Bde. D Coy for work with the 8th Bde. After started for Battalion war diary. D Coy shut back again Coy orders 1 G.O.C 76th Inf. Bde. moving to active operations on our left front.	
Tilloy	25/4/17	10 p.m.	A.B.C. Coy wired length of 650 yds. Shrapnel trench. D. Coy wired 200 yds. on eastern outskirts of Tilloy.	
Tilloy	26/4/17	12 m.n.	A.B.C. Coys. continued wiring of Shrapnel trench and also from junction Shrapnel trench and Aween. O.U.6.5.6. They wired Balfront 650 yds. D. Coy wired of Trench running from about O.12.b.7. due East to Shrapnel trench	
Tilloy	28/4/17	2 a.m.	A. B. C. Coys continued wiring same sector as for 26th inst. D. Coy completed wiring trench started night 26th inst. and 100 yds. due east from O.I.d.6.7. work was hampered considerably by very heavy B attachm. shell-fire.	
Tilloy	29/4/17	6 p.m.	The notes under orders G.O.C. 3rd Division.	
Tilloy	29/4/17	6 p.m.	A+B Coys dug C.T. from north of Shrapnel tr. to Front Line 4.30 yds. C Coy completed wiring Shrapnel 2.30 yds. D.Y Coy completed wiring Reserve Line.	R. Ryf. Kerr Lt. Col. (O/C)

20th (S.) Batt. King's Royal Rifle Corps. (Pioneer).

Vol XI

War Diary

Volume XII

From 1st May 1917
To 31st May 1917

Army Form C. 2118.

WAR DIARY
or
INTELLIGENCE SUMMARY.
(Erase heading not required.)

Instructions regarding War Diaries and Intelligence Summaries are contained in F. S. Regs., Part II. and the Staff Manual respectively. Title pages will be prepared in manuscript.

Place	Date	Hour	Summary of Events and Information	Remarks and references to Appendices
Lilly	1/5/17	6 p.m.	A, B, & C Coys. set out to dig French Line Trench from Arrowhead Copse to Pot Line. Enemy known to the Enemy moved forward no troops was trouble. D Coy connected up all holes to form an Assembly Trench for a distance of about 400 yds.	
Lilly	2/5/17	6 p.m.	The Battn. moved its position to trenches about 400 yds due North of Lilly. They rested preparatory to attack.	
Lilly	3/5/17	6 p.m.	The Battn. stood by all day but were not called out.	
Lilly	4/5/17	6 p.m.	The Battalion was called upon to dig a Line Trench north of March from O.1.d.6.8 to O.1.a.6.7. They dug the full length about 900 yds. to a depth of 4'.	
Lilly	5/5/17	6 p.m.	The Battalion continued work on above Line Trench. Deepening, drawing, and Trebling Trenchwork where necessary.	
Lilly	6/5/17	6 p.m.	Continued work on above Line Trench.	
Lilly	7/5/17	6 p.m.	Continued work on above Line Trench.	
Lilly	8/5/17	6 p.m.	A & B Coys continued work on Eastern sector of above trench. B Coy dug 300 yds Line Trench due west of Orchard Trench. C Coy. moved the new sector dug by B Coy.	R.L.

Army Form C. 2118.

WAR DIARY
or
INTELLIGENCE SUMMARY.
(Erase heading not required.)

Instructions regarding War Diaries and Intelligence Summaries are contained in F. S. Regs., Part II. and the Staff Manual respectively. Title pages will be prepared in manuscript.

Place	Date	Hour	Summary of Events and Information	Remarks and references to Appendices
Lilly	9/3/17	6 p.m.	The Battalion continued work on same section of trench as for 8th inst. Fire-stepping, building parapet, deepening &c.	
Lilly	10/3/17	6 p.m.	A & D Coys. carried on with work as for 9th inst. B & C Coys. were engaged widening and deepening Carnotes Trench.	
Lilly	11/3/17	6 p.m.	The Coy. carried on with same work as for 10th inst.	
Lilly	12/3/17	6 p.m.	A, B, C Coys. cleared old German C.T. from I.34.c.9.3 to N.5.2.3.5. D. Coy. rested preparatory to being used by 76th Bde. in operations.	
Lilly	13/3/17	6 p.m.	A & B. Coys. continued work on Vine trench. They cleared 400 yds from junction of East and Hope trenches, working westward south of Monchy. Dannel to 12th Div. C.T. "C" Coy. a C.T. from western end of trench and rented out work on the "D" Coy. got up to site of work but could not work as the attack failed.	
Lilly	14/3/17	6 p.m.	A. & D. Coys. continued work on East French. C. Coy. continued work on new C.T. B. Coy. continued work on Vine Lane.	
Agnes-lea Hussars	15/3/17	6 p.m.	The B. attalion moved into Talavera Camp night 14th inst. move being completed by 12 m.n. Coys. spent the day cleaning up the new generally.	

Army Form C. 2118.

WAR DIARY
or
INTELLIGENCE SUMMARY.
(Erase heading not required.)

Instructions regarding War Diaries and Intelligence Summaries are contained in F. S. Regs., Part II. and the Staff Manual respectively. Title pages will be prepared in manuscript.

Place	Date	Hour	Summary of Events and Information	Remarks and references to Appendices
Arras	16/5/17	6 p.m.	Battalion moved into Arras as Corps Reserve; move completed by 4 p.m.	
Arras	17/5/17	6 p.m.	VI Corps held not order any work to be done, reorganization of Battalion commenced.	
Arras	18/5/17	6 p.m.	Reorganization and training carried on.	
Arras	19/5/17	6 p.m.	As for 18th inst.	
Arras	20/5/17	6 p.m.	As for 19th inst.	
Arras	21/5/17	6 p.m.	As for 20th inst.	
Liencourt	22/5/17	6 p.m.	73 battalion moved to Liencourt; move complete by 3.35 p.m.	
Liencourt	23/5/17	6 p.m.	All ranks were employed in Infantry training during morning and organized games afternoon.	
Liencourt	24/5/17	6 p.m.	As for 23rd inst.	
Liencourt	25/5/17	6 p.m.	As for 24th inst.	
Liencourt	26/5/17	6 p.m.	As for 25th inst.	
Liencourt	27/5/17	6 p.m.	Church parade morning; remainder of day free.	
Liencourt	28/5/17	6 p.m.	Continued training as for last week.	
Liencourt	29/5/17	6 p.m.	Continued training as for 28th inst.	

Army Form C. 2118.

WAR DIARY
or
INTELLIGENCE SUMMARY.
(Erase heading not required.)

Instructions regarding War Diaries and Intelligence Summaries are contained in F. S. Regs., Part II. and the Staff Manual respectively. Title pages will be prepared in manuscript.

Place	Date	Hour	Summary of Events and Information	Remarks and references to Appendices
Lincourt	30/5/17	6 p.m.	Continued training as for 29th inst.	
Lincourt	31/5/17	6 p.m.	Continued training as for 30th inst.	

Field
1/6/17

F. Hyde Lt. Cl.
Comg. 20 KRRC

K.R.2278/ From O.C. 20th KRRC. K.R.74.
          to "Q" 3rd Division.

                Herewith War Diary
for June 1917. Please acknowledge
receipt herein.

                        R Inglis Lt. Col.
                        Comg. 20' KRRC
Field.
30/6/17

WAR DIARY
or
INTELLIGENCE SUMMARY.

(Erase heading not required.)

Army Form C. 2118.

20 K.R.R.C. (P) P/3

Place	Date	Hour	Summary of Events and Information	Remarks and references to Appendices
Liencourt	1/6/17	6p.m.	Continued training during morning, organized games afternoon	
Tilloy	2/6/17	6p.m.	Moved by bus from Liencourt to Boisieux, marched to Tilloy and occupied front system of trenches. More completed by 12.30 p.m.	
Tilloy	3/6/17	6p.m.	Companies started work in sector named Monchy. 'A' Coy started work on C.T. (connecting Staffs and front trenches) that led to Bit Lane. 'B' Coy started work connecting 200 yds long line from front trench westward with a file trench. 'C' Coy started work connecting trench with a file trench orchard trench from Stenvan Lane towards Bit Lane.	
Tilloy	4/6/17	6p.m.	All Coys. continued work in for 3rd inst.	
Tilloy	5/6/17	6p.m.	All Coys. continued work as for 4th inst.	
Tilloy	6/6/17	6p.m.	All Coys. continued work as for 5th inst.	
Tilloy	7/6/17	6p.m.	All Coys. continued work as for 6th inst. 'D' Coy completed obstacle between Stenvan and Bit Lane.	S/1

Army Form C. 2118.

WAR DIARY
or
INTELLIGENCE SUMMARY.
(Erase heading not required.)

Instructions regarding War Diaries and Intelligence Summaries are contained in F.S. Regs., Part II. and the Staff Manual respectively. Title pages will be prepared in manuscript.

Place	Date	Hour	Summary of Events and Information	Remarks and references to Appendices
Jilloy	8/6/17	6 p.m.	A & D Coys continued work sandbagging, deepening and draining Brickson Lane. B. Coy continued firestepping Vine Lane, and commenced wiring South side.	
Jilloy	9/6/17	6 p.m.	C. Coy continued firestepping Orchard West. Coys continued work as for 8th inst.	
Jilloy	10/6/17	6 p.m.	Coys continued work as for 9th inst.	
Jilloy	11/6/17	6 p.m.	Coys continued work as for 10th inst.	
Jilloy	12/6/17	6 p.m.	Coys continued work as for 11th inst, with the exception of D Coy who commenced wiring East trench.	
Jilloy	13/6/17	6 p.m.	All Coys continued work as for 12th inst.	
Jilloy	14/6/17	6 p.m.	All Coys continued work as for 13th inst.	
Jilloy	15/6/17	6 p.m.	"A" Coy continued work on Brickson Lane. "D" and "B" Coy worked at clearing and French trenching Vine Lane. C and "B" Coy rendezvoused at the cave at La Tour Farm preparatory to being used for work in 76th Bde. operations.	C.V.

A5834 Wt.W4973/M687 750,000 8/16 D. D. & L. Ltd. Forms/C.2113/13.

Army Form C. 2118.

WAR DIARY
or
INTELLIGENCE SUMMARY.
(Erase heading not required.)

Instructions regarding War Diaries and Intelligence Summaries are contained in F. S. Regs., Part II. and the Staff Manual respectively. Title pages will be prepared in manuscript.

Place	Date	Hour	Summary of Events and Information	Remarks and references to Appendices
Lilly	16/6/17	6 p.m.	C and 2 B Coys. and 2 C.T.'s connecting Hoop and Hill trenches. They manned the trenches during Counter attack and helped to repel same. A Coy. worked on the clearing of Oats trench, and D on the clearing of Grape trench.	
Lilly	17/6/17	6 p.m.	A Coy. continued work of clearing Pick trench. B C.D. Coys. cleared Grape trench and part of Vine Lane.	
Lilly	18/6/17	6 p.m.	B + C Coys. continued work widening and deepening his new C.T.'s during the German counter attack they manned Hoop trench and helped the Suffolks to repel the same. A + D Coys. continued work clearing Vine Lane.	
Lilly	19/6/17	6 p.m.	A + D Coys. day & trench connecting Hoop & thus trenches. B + C Coys. continued work clearing Vine Lane. In the afternoon moved into Arras for the night the Battalion	
Lattre St Quentin	20/6/17	6 p.m.	The Battalion marched to Lattre St Quentin the move being completed by 10 a.m.	
Denier	21/6/17	6 p.m.	The Battalion marched to Denier, the move being completed by 10 a.m.	

WAR DIARY
or
INTELLIGENCE SUMMARY.
(Erase heading not required.)

Army Form C. 2118.

Place	Date	Hour	Summary of Events and Information	Remarks and references to Appendices
Denier	22/6/17	6pm	The day was spent in reorganizing the Battalion into Platoons and Sections and in cleaning up generally	
Denier	23/6/17	6pm	The Battalion started training, hereby its day in infantry training	
Denier	24/6/17	6pm	The Battalion rested, Sunday	
Denier	25/6/17	6pm	Training was continued. General Infantry training morning, and specialist training afternoon.	
Denier	26/6/17	6pm	Training was continued as for 25th inst.	
Denier	27/6/17	6pm	Evening was continued as for 26th inst.	
Gouches	28/6/17	6pm	The Battalion marched from Denier to Gouches, move being completed by 12 noon.	
Gouches	29/6/17	6pm	Training was continued, chiefly Pioneer work	
Gouches	30/6/17	6pm	Pioneer training was continued as for 29th inst.	

R. Wylie Lt
Comg 20

From OC 20th KRRC
To 3rd Division Q.

Herewith War Diary 20th KRRC
(Pioneers) please,

31-7-17

J. Jenkins Major
Comg 20th KRRC

War Diary
20th Kings Royal Rifles
(Pioneers)

1st to 31st July 1917.

Army Form C. 2118.

WAR DIARY
or
INTELLIGENCE SUMMARY.
(Erase heading not required.)

Instructions regarding War Diaries and Intelligence Summaries are contained in F. S. Regs., Part II. and the Staff Manual respectively. Title pages will be prepared in manuscript.

Place	Date	Hour	Summary of Events and Information	Remarks and references to Appendices
Mory Achiet-le-Petit	1/7/17	6 p.m.	The Battalion moved by road and rail to Achiet-le-Petit, being completed by 2.20 p.m.	
Achiet-le-Petit	2/7/17	6 p.m.	The Battalion carried on with training during afternoon.	
Nr. Haplincourt	3/7/17	10 p.m.	The Battalion relieved the 5th Sussex Pioneers, relief being completed by 10 p.m.	
Nr. Haplincourt	4/7/17	6 p.m.	The Battalion rested.	
Nr. Haplincourt	5/7/17	6 p.m.	Officers and N.C.O's thoroughly reconnoitred new sector of line taken over.	
Nr. Haplincourt	6/7/17	6 p.m.	All Coys started wiring the Front Line; 600 yds of thick entanglement was completed.	
Nr. Haplincourt	7/7/17	6 p.m.	All Coys continued wiring the front line; about 620 yds of thick entanglement was completed.	
Nr. Haplincourt	8/7/17	6 p.m.	All Coys continued wiring front line; about 620 yds of thick entanglement completed.	

Army Form C. 2118.

WAR DIARY
or
INTELLIGENCE SUMMARY.
(Erase heading not required.)

Place	Date	Hour	Summary of Events and Information	Remarks and references to Appendices
Lebucquire	9/7/17	6p.m.	Batt. Hd. Qrs. moved to Lebucquire as an Hd. to nearer Coy. and work on Coy. continued. Wiring Front Line 650 yds being completed.	
Lebucquire	10/7/17	6p.m.	All Coys continued wiring Front Line 690 yds. of wire being completed.	
Lebucquire	11/7/17	6p.m.	Wiring of Front Line continued; distance completed 650 yds.	
Lebucquire	12/7/17	6p.m.	Wiring of Front Line continued; distance completed 590 yds.	
Lebucquire	13/7/17	6p.m.	Wiring of Front Line continued; distance completed 660 yds.	
Lebucquire	14/7/17	6p.m.	Wiring of Front Line continued. A Coy thickened 300 yds. of wire previously erected. B.C. & D Coys erected about 450 yds. of new entanglement.	
Lebucquire	15/7/17	6p.m.	Wiring of Front Line continued. A Coy thickened 300 yds. of wire previously erected, and B.C. & D Coys erected about 400 yds. of new entanglement.	
Lebucquire	16/7/17	6p.m.	Wiring of Front Line continued. A Coy thickened 300 yds. of wire previously erected, and B.C. & D Coys erected about 480 yds. of new entanglement.	
Lebucquire	17/7/17	6p.m.	Wiring of Front Line continued by all Coys; about 600 yds. I think entanglement erected.	
Lebucquire	18/7/17	6p.m.	Wiring of Front Line continued by A.B.C. Coys; distance wired 430 yds. D Coy were unable to work owing to special Patrol work by Infantry.	
Lebucquire	19/7/17	6p.m.	Wiring of Front Line continued by all Coys; distance wired 490 yds.	C.L.

Army Form C. 2118.

WAR DIARY
or
INTELLIGENCE SUMMARY.
(Erase heading not required.)

Instructions regarding War Diaries and Intelligence Summaries are contained in F. S. Regs., Part II. and the Staff Manual respectively. Title pages will be prepared in manuscript.

Place	Date	Hour	Summary of Events and Information	Remarks and references to Appendices
Colincamps	20.7.17	6pm	Wiring of front line continued by all Coys distance wired 390 yds	
"	21.7.17	6pm	Wiring of front line continued " " " " 450 yds	
"	22.7.17	6pm	Wiring of front line continued by all Coys distance wired 465 "	
"	23.7.17	6pm	Wiring of front line continued by all Coys distance wired 470 "	
"	24.7.17	6pm	Wiring of front line continued by all Coys distance wired 490 "	
"	25.7.17	6pm	Wiring of front line continued by all Coys distance wired 370 "	
"	26.7.17	6pm	Wiring of front line continued by all Coys distance wired 300 "	
"	26.7.17	6pm	Wiring of front line continued by all Coys distance wired 480 "	
"	27.7.17	6pm	Wiring of front line continued by all Coys distance wired 600 "	
"	28.7.17	6pm	Wiring of front line continued by all Coys distance wired 500 "	
"	29.7.17	6pm	Wiring of front line continued by all Coys distance wired 540 "	
"	30.7.17	6pm	Wiring of front line continued by all Coys distance wired 175 "	
"	31.7.17	6pm	Wiring of front line continued by A & D Coy distance wired 175 " Intermediate line & improvement of Posts & making of dug outs commenced distance wired 150 yds	

J Jenkins Major
Comdg 10th KRRC

9214

20th (S) Bn. K.R.R.C. (Pioneers)

War Diary - August 1917.

Confidential   K 10

3rd Division Q.

Herewith War Diary for
August 1917.

31-8-17   J Jenkins Lt Col
                     Comg 3d KRRC

7th Inverness (Pioneers)

Army Form C. 2118.

WAR DIARY
or
INTELLIGENCE SUMMARY.
(Erase heading not required.)

Place	Date	Hour	Summary of Events and Information	Remarks and references to Appendices
Rubrouquin	1-8-17	6pm	All Companies at work on the Intermediate Line. Improving Posts, revetting firestep & constructing dug outs, and improving safety & erecting new wire.	
do	2-8-17	6pm	Continued work on the Intermediate Line	
do	3-8-17	6pm	Continued work on the Intermediate Line	
do	4-8-17	6pm	A & B Coys continued work on the Intermediate Line. C & D. Coys were relieved by another Bgde on the morning on the 4th. "C" Coy resting, D Coy moved to Siewicourt.	
do	5-8-17	6pm	A & B Coys continued work on the Intermediate Line. C Coy rested. D. Coy commenced work taking down huts at Lefebr army camp and re-erecting them for use of S.H.Q.	
do	6-8-17	8pm	A & B Coys continued work on the Intermediate Line. C Coy rested. D. Coy continued work of taking and re-erecting Huts for S.H.Q.	
do	7-8-17	6pm	A Coy continued work on the Intermediate Line till 8pm, when they were relieved by C.Q. B Coy continued work on the Intermediate Line, to be relieved A Coy on the Intermediate line at 9pm. D Coy continued work on Huts.	
do	8-8-17	6pm	A Coy resting. B & C Coy continued work on the Intermediate Line. D Coy continued work	
do	9-8-17	6pm	B & C Coy continued work on the Intermediate Line. D Coy erected new scatter sheets and 225 galvanised A Coy continued digging the first line from Post 4, into new scatter sheets	
do	10-7-17	6pm	A Coy continued working if front Line 225 X garvenneated. B & C Coy continued work on Intermediate Line. D Coy continued work on Huts.	

Army Form C. 2118.

WAR DIARY
or
INTELLIGENCE SUMMARY.
(Erase heading not required.)

Place	Date	Hour	Summary of Events and Information	Remarks and references to Appendices
Laburquière	11.8.17	6 pm	A Coy continued revision of front line 253 x spans erected. B + C Coy continued work on battlements line. B + C Coy continued work on huts.	
Laburquière	12.8.17	6 pm	A Coy continued revision of front line 200 ft of wire erected. B+C Coys continued work on huts. D Coy continued work on huts.	
do	13.8.17	6 pm	A Coy continued revision of front line. 230 x spans erected. B + C Coy continued work on huts.	
do	14.8.17	6 pm	A Coy continued revision of front line. 235 x spans erected. Wiring pgs. no. 11 + 13. B+C Coy continued work on huts.	
do	15.8.17	6 pm	A, B, C Coys continued revision of front line. 235 x spans erected. Revising pgs no. 12 + 14.	
do	16.8.17	6 pm	A, B Coy continued revision of front line. 235 x spans erected. Revising pgs no. 13 + 15.	
do	17.8.17	6 pm	A, B Coy continued revision of front line. 235 x spans erected. Revising pgs no. 14 + 16.	
do	18.8.17	6 pm	A Coy completed revision of front line 30 x spans erected. Revising pgs no. 15 + 17.	
do	19.8.17	6 pm	A Coy commenced work on intermediate line. dug outs, drains and repairing timber erecting post. Revising pgs no. for 18th.	
do	20.8.17	6 pm	All Coys continued work as on 19th.	
do	21.8.17	6 pm	All Coys continued work as on 20th.	
do	22.8.17	6 pm	All Coys continued work as on 21st.	
do	23.8.17	6 pm	All Coys continued work as on 2pm up to 3 pm, when A, B Coys were withdrawn to be used on readiness for physical parade made up of 9th Brigade.	
at	24.8.17	6 pm	A, B, C Coys not being required by 9th Brigade, commenced work again at 4 pm on the dug outs, wiring etc. to the battalion line. D Coy continued work on huts at Sept 8.	

90th / RECC (River)

Army Form C. 2118.

WAR DIARY
or
INTELLIGENCE SUMMARY.
(Erase heading not required.)

Place	Date	Hour	Summary of Events and Information	Remarks and references to Appendices
Fabrugures	25.8.17	6pm	A, B & C Coy continued work on Posts in the Intermediate Line. Dug into mining & deepening trenches, revetting firesteps etc. D Coy continued work on Huts at new Stn Qrs.	
— do —	26.8.17	6pm	A, B & C Coy continued work as on 25th. D Coy less 1 Platoon continued work on Stn Qrs. 1 Platoon of D Coy proceeded to Beaumetz to prepare billets for Coy.	
— do —	27.8.17	6pm	All Coys continued work as on 26th. The 2.5.8 T.C. R.E. 176th and Drys unit in Posts 144,34, from B Coy respectively. By Armitage 4 S.S. 4.T.B. joined Battn.	
— do —	28.8.17	6pm	All Coys continued work as on 27th.	
— do —	29.8.17	6pm	All Coys continued work as on 28th. One Platoon of D Coy proceeded to Beaumetz to prepare billets.	
— do —	30.8.17	6pm	All Coys continued work as on 29th. 11 Reinforcements arrived.	
— do —	31.8.17	6pm	A, B & C Coys continued work as on 30th. Remainder of D Coy proceeded to Beaumetz.	

J. Jenkins Lt. Col.
Comdg. 90th R.E.C.C.

K.F.76

<u>CONFIDENTIAL</u>

From O.C 20th K.R.R.C (Pioneers)
To 3rd Division Q

Herewith War Diary for September please.

J Jenkins Lieut. Col.
Commanding 20th
K.R.R.C

Field
1.10.17

WAR DIARY or INTELLIGENCE SUMMARY

Army Form C. 2118.

20th R.R. 16/1/15

Place	Date	Hour	Summary of Events and Information	Remarks and references to Appendices
Rubempré	1-9-17	6pm	A B & C Coy continued work on the Intermediate Line. D. Coy prepared billets in Beaumetz and cleared Road running past Billets.	
"	2-9-17	6pm	A B & C Coy continued work as on 1st. D. Coy working on Roads clearing, scraping and repairing between Beaumetz and Cambrai Rd. and between Beaumetz and Doignies, except one Platoon employed in making drains for draining of Road at I. 30.2.2.7. S.t. 4 & W.e. 4 & B.R.E.	
"	3-9-17	6pm	A B & C continued work as on 2nd. D Coy. 3 Platoons draining road & 1 Platoon repairing road.	
"	4-9-17	6pm	All Coys continued work as on 3rd.	
"	4-9-17	6pm	All Coys continued work and were concentrated in Camp.	
Bastincourt	5-9-17	6pm	Battalion moved to BERTINCOURT	
"	6-9-17	6pm	All Coys employed on drainage scheme, clearing ditch digging new trench where required & putting in Front Slabs, & bridging where required.	
— do —	7-9-17	6pm	All Coys continued work as on 6th	
— do —	8-9-17	6pm	All Coys continued work as on 7th	
— do —	9-9-17	6pm	Resting	
— do —	10-9-17	6pm	All Coys commenced Training, particular attention being paid to Musketry & Bayonet fighting	
— do —	11-9-17	6pm	All Coys training	
— do —	12-9-17	6pm	All Coys training	

Army Form C. 2118.

WAR DIARY
or
INTELLIGENCE SUMMARY.
(Erase heading not required.)

Instructions regarding War Diaries and Intelligence Summaries are contained in F. S. Regs., Part II. and the Staff Manual respectively. Title pages will be prepared in manuscript.

Place	Date	Hour	Summary of Events and Information	Remarks and references to Appendices
Berthcourt	13.9.17	6pm	All Coys continued Training	
— do —	14.9.17	6pm	All Coys continued Training	
— do —	15.9.17	6pm	Bath. Continued Training (Completion of Platoon assault exercise shortly). Rapid Slow shooting, Lewis gun, including firing of assault arms, Transport, Lewis & all other Movements.	
Achiet le Petit	16.9.17	6pm	Battalion marched from Berthincourt to Achiet le Petit.	
— do —	17.9.17	6pm	All Coys training	
— do —	18.9.17	12 noon	Preparing to entrain for HOPOUTRE.	
Watou	19.9.17	6pm	Entrained at Mirraumont at 3pm & proceeded to HOPOUTRE, arriving at 3am. Detrained and marched to REAY Camp near WATOU, arriving at 5am.	
— do —	20.9.17	6pm	All Coys Training.	
Watou	21.9.17	12 noon	Preparing for move to YPRES.	
YPRES	22.9.17	6pm	Battn moved into new Camp No 2, at YPRES South. Work reconnoitred by Officers.	
— do —	23.9.17	6pm	A Coys were employed in making a good track for Infantry, filling in shell holes & using frames & shell boards where necessary. B Coy Employed under 435 Fd Coy R.E. Making a bridge & carrying Tanks, Putting a Ramp & carrying Materials. C Coy Carrying No 2 Mule Track making Infantry Track. D Coy Making 9 Shoes for bivouacs on POTIZE - ZONNEBEKE road.	
— do —	24.9.17	6pm	All Coys working as on 23rd except C Coy who were employed carrying bundles of wood	
— do —	25.9.17	6pm	All Coys working as on 23rd.	
— do —	26.9.17	4pm	All Coys awaiting orders to proceed to work on consolidation etc	

WAR DIARY
or
INTELLIGENCE SUMMARY.
(Erase heading not required.)

Army Form C. 2118.

Place	Date	Hour	Summary of Events and Information	Remarks and references to Appendices
YPRES	27/4/17	4pm	A Coy. & Platoon went out to the new lines to reconnoitre the front line to be taken over. 1 & 4 Platoons of this Coy. were employed 4.0-7.30 p.m. digging Y3 Area well under HOLLEBEKE. MN. 3 Platoon & MN 3 Platoon were employed making fascines.	
		10am	When they came and took to Camp.	
			B.Coy were attached to R.E. & left for making strong points. They were sent up about 12.30 am & made a strong point under instructions from Section of 56 Coy R.E. 10 pioneers were killed & 9 wounded. 2 Sgts & 1 Pvt killed & 24 O.R. including 3 Sgts wounded.	
			C.Coy were attached to y/6 Lt Hy Bde for making strong points. They were sent up about 2 hrs but were unable to commence work until 1am. They made a defensive position on the front line at ZONNEBEKE by family's with Robin & putting up wire consisting of barbed concertina wire. The work was completed.	
			D.Coy were employed in making 9' track for infantry on the YPRES - ZONNEBEKE road, & widely different & 2 Platoons of A Coy were engaged in widening the Track in the 70m Line. 3 Platoon & 1 Platoon with 2 Section of C.Coy.	
— do —	28.4.17	6pm	ZONNEBEKE road. Together with 2 Section of C.Coy B.Coy were employed making strong points over the Moraine of the STEENBEEKE near BESTIN FARM. 4 Track, were constructing ways from 58 x 108 with the aid of hurdles & French 13 inch. C.Coy. 2 Platoons were employed with the 76' Bgde in constructing strong point on New Front Line 3 Platoon were employed on Road work with A Coy as above. D.Coy resting. They did not return to Camp until 11 pm. A.Coy working on ZONNEBEKE road continuing to 18:1. B.Coy completed track on the STEENBEKE	
— do —	29.4.17	6pm	Moraine commenced 28th. C.Coy repairing & laying new Duck Board across on northern breakwater Track towards SN & SOUEZ. D.Coy making 9' track on YPRES - ZONNEBEKE road.	
— do —	30.4.17	6pm	All Coys working in 29th except B.Coy who were employed laying Rad Road on 9' Track.	

J. Jenkins Lt Col
Commdg 217/Pioneers

M.24.

From O.C.
  20th King's Royal Rifles   In the field
                                  1st Oct. 17.
To   Q
      3rd Division

Attached war Diary A.F.C.2118

for the month of October

                        Chinnall Martin
                              Lt. Col.
                        Comdg.
                          20 K.R.R.C.

P/ 20 K.R.R.C
Vol 16

WAR DIARY or INTELLIGENCE SUMMARY
(Erase heading not required.)

Army Form C. 2118.

Place	Date	Hour	Summary of Events and Information	Remarks and references to Appendices
Brandhoek	1-10-17	6pm	B. Coy continued work on J. Track laying duckboards. C. Coy continued work on Northern duckwalk. Track laying stands bombing instruction etc. A & D Coy were sent to Frezenberg Ridge to make an artillery track. This task was completed.	
–do–	2-10-17	12 noon	Batt. moved to No 7 Camp Brandhoek.	
–do–	3-10-17	10 am	Batt. preparing for move to Winnezeele. Transport sent by road at 7.45 am. Batt. arrived at No 3 Winnezeele Area No. 3. – Major C.R. Martin took over command of Battalion	
–do–	4-10-17	6pm	Batt. moved to Balenberg and came under the orders of V Corps.	
Buysscheure	5-10-17	5pm	Coys training & musketry, kits etc.	
"	6-10-17	6pm	All company training	Special class for N.C.O's & Lewis gunners
"	7-10-17	6pm	Church parade –	
"	8-10-17	6pm	Coy training continued	Special class for NCO's & Lewis gunners
Elverdinghe	9-10-17	6pm	Battalion moved at 9pm to Siege Camp arrived 2 am by busses – Transport by road arrived 10 pm. Under arrangements	
Canal Bank C.25 central.	10-10-17	6pm	Battalion moved to Canal Bank arriving 5 pm. L.T.M. & Transport to Marsh Farm – attacked 6 Battalions	
"	11-10-17	6pm	Companies took over from 2 K.R.R. & 9 Division. A Coy exploratory Alberta Bank front down 150 x men each – B Coy Support Moustrap to Hugel Tirpitz Farm, front down 150 x men each. C Coy front area	
"	12-10-17	6pm	A & B Coy continued work –	
"	13-10-17	6pm	support wait here Triangle to Hubner Fm. D Coy carrying parties as laid down for 6 Coys French.	
"	14-10-17	6pm	A B & D Coys continued work at C.21 & at – Eighty 9.2 dugouts taking up material	
"	15-10-17	6pm	A B C & D Coys continued work as for 13 inst.	
"	16-10-17	6pm	B & D Coys worked on Springfield – Frezen ... road Artillery Road falling in shell holes 6 m/h C Coy staining platforms Triangle Road for slabing – Triangle Road.	
"	17-10-17	6pm	A & B Coys contributing and laying out to be lifted out. C Coy continued work on Springfield E of Springfield Road	
"	18-10-17	6pm	B & D Coys completed R.E. bunker under Springfield Rd	
"	19-10-17	6pm	A & C Coys completed Rd bunkers Everett & Jackson. Rd slabbing being driven up several times by holed shelling	

WAR DIARY or INTELLIGENCE SUMMARY.

Army Form C. 2118.

Instructions regarding War Diaries and Intelligence Summaries are contained in F.S. Regs., Part II. and the Staff Manual respectively. Title pages will be prepared in manuscript.

(Erase heading not required.)

Place	Date	Hour	Summary of Events and Information	Remarks and references to Appendices
CANAL BANK C 25 central	18.10.17	6 p.m.	D Coy preparing formation for tram line from HAUBNER FARM to YORK HOUSE. C Coy strengthening & backing shelly floor on SPRINGFIELD horse line. B Coy cleaning & mending rd SPRINGFIELD Rd	
do.	19.10.17	6 p.m.	A & D Coy continued work on HAUBNER farm line. B & C Coy continued work on SPRINGFIELD ROAD	
do.	20.10.17	6 p.m.	A Coy continued work as for 19th. B Coy on SPRINGFIELD ROAD. C & D Coy on trams - men taken from HAUBNER SPOT FARM and widening track of existing lines from TRIANGLE to WINNIPEG. For R.F.A.	
do.	21.10.17	6 p.m.	A & B Coy continued work on SPRINGFIELD ROAD, potholes, etc. C & D Coy continued work on two light railway lines from SPOT FARM - 200 x of prov[] & 200 yd hand laid. 15 min[] men for Gage[] pit in 12 [] for R.F.A. mch [] positions	
do.	22.10.17	6 p.m.	All Coys continued work as for 21st. 150 x of line completed	
do.	23.10.17	6 p.m.	Work continued as for 22nd. Heavy hostile shelling harassed work and destroyed a considerable portion of materials	
do.	24.10.17	6 p.m.	Work continued after 2330. 6th Division took over from 3rd Division	
do.	25.10.17	6 p.m.	Carrier [] on [] of 18th Divn. Baths in reserve & [] of []	
do.	26.10.17	3 p.m.	Battalion resting, awaiting move from 18th Divn.	
do.	27.10.17	6 p.m.	Orders received from 18th Corps to [] R.HAIGAN and take over camps of 18th Royal Warwickshires. Trenches. Advance party went to DAWSONS CORNER.	
DAWSONS CORNER B.22.d central	28.10.17	6 p.m.	Battalion moved to DAWSONS CORNER. H.22.d. central, took over work of R.N.Fus. Light railway and 30.d.87. A.D.L.R. 5 Army.	
do.	29.10.17	6 p.m.	2 Officers 100 OR at KEMPTON PARK laying & fixing rail, and making embankments. 1 Officer 50 OR on WELCH SPUR widening & mending formation for new line. 2 Officers 100 OR at PLYMOUTH JUNC. work on switches thro' of B LINE & B15 LINE. 1 [] 25 OR on ADMIRAL SPUR - Ballasting & backing - raised lines 6". 2 [] 75 OR on MAIN LINE - Ballasting & backing. 30 yd rail on embankment through CANAL prepared. Drainage 500 x 27 centre track.	
do.	30.10.17	6 p.m.	1 [] 50 OR on HINDENBERG LOOP - preparing drainage 50 x of line & backing & banking 120 x.	
do.	31.10.17	6 p.m.	Work continued as for 29. repaired blocks & buffers of track at DICK KERR SIDING. Circular letter received from 32 Divn - attached copy. Work continued as for 29.	

Col. Trenter
Lt. Col.
Comg. 24 Kings Royal Rifles

War Diary Copy

3rd Division A/3072.

The G.O.C. 3rd Division has much pleasure in circulating to all units of the Division the following letter which he has received from the G.O.C. 9th Division.

The fine spirit of co-operation displayed by the 20th Battn. K.R.R.Corps whilst attached to the 9th Division is, the G.O.C. well knows, typical of all units of the 3rd Division.

"I desire to express my high appreciation of the good work done by the 20th (Pioneer) Battalion K.R.R. during the time it has been attached to the 9th Division.

Willing, hardworking and cheery, I regard myself as fortunate in having had the services of such a fine Battalion placed at my disposal."

27th October, 1917.

(Signed) R.H. Collins, Lt.Col.,
A.A. & Q.M.G., 3rd Division.

M.K.0

From   O.C.   In the field
       20th King's Royal Rifles   3 Dec. 17

To.   Q
       3rd Division

Attached War Diary A.F. C2118
for the month of November.

                           C. Roswell Martin
                                    Lt Col
                    Comdg.
                           20th K.R.R.C.

WAR DIARY
or
INTELLIGENCE SUMMARY.
(Erase heading not required.)

Army Form C. 2118.

20 K R R C
1/11/17

Place	Date	Hour	Summary of Events and Information	Remarks and references to Appendices
DAWSONS CORNER B.22.d. Central	1.11.17	6pm	Continued work on Light Railways from CANAL BANK to POLECAPPLE - ST JULIAN Rd	
	2.11.17	6pm	Continued work as for 1.1b	
	3.11.17	6pm	do	
	4.11.17	6pm	do	
HOUTKERQUE CAUDESCURE	5.11.17	6pm	The battalion moved from DAWSONS CORNER to HOUTKERQUE. Move completed 3.30pm	
	6.11.17	6pm	The battalion marched from HOUTKERQUE to LA MOTTE area, starting at 8.45 marched via STEENVOORDE - HAZEBROUCK - LA MOTTE arriving 5pm. Distance 26 miles. Billeted via MERVILLE	
GONNEHAM	7.11.17	6pm	The battalion marched from CAUDESCURE to GONNEHAM. starting at 9.30am marched via MERVILLE	
HERSIN.	8.11.17	6pm	ROBICQUE - GONNEHAM arriving 3pm. Trunk continued from Houtkerque. GONNEHAM to HERSIN via OBLINHAM - BETHUNE - NŒUX-LES-MINES - HERSIN - starting at 9.15am arrived HERSIN at 3.45pm	
ARRAS.	9.11.17	6pm	Continued march to ARRAS. via GRAND SERVINS. VILLERS. AU BOIS - CHAUSSE - ST CATHERINES - ARRAS. Started 8.30am arrived ARRAS 3pm.	
BEUGNATRE.	10.11.17	6pm	Marched from ARRAS to rejoin 3rd DIV at FAVREUIL - marched from ARRAS at 9am via BOYELLES - ERVILLERS - SAPIGNEY - passed DHQ at 2.30pm. arrived camp at BEUGNATRE - SUCERIE Rd at 3pm.	A fresh Battle
	11.11.17	6pm	Cleaning up. making camp comfortable	
	12.11.17	6pm	Resting. making camp comfortable	
	13.11.17	6pm	A + D Coys Working on emplacement of SUCERIE - ECOUST. BULLECOURT Rd. making Hobnob room) Cradles in ECOUST and on BULLECOURT Rd - B Coy working on NOREUIL - VAULX Rd draining and making dug outs. C Coy wiring support line in front of STANHOPE REDOUT	
	14.11.17	6pm	work continued as for 13.L	
	15.11.17	6pm	do	
	16.11.17	6pm	do	
	17.11.17	6pm	do	
	18.11.17	6pm	do	
	19.11.17	6pm	A.B. D Coys continued work as for 13. C Coy employed laying v. lights metal on roads + taking slabs from dump at ECOUST. 60 slabs placed (Nath. S of BULLECOURT	
	20.11.17	6pm	A + D Coys started work dump Bullecourt. B + C Coy Laboring road from ECOUST dump to BULLECOURT	
	21.11.17	6pm	Work continued as for 20.L	
	22.11.17	6pm	Work continued as for 21.L 700 slabs brought through ECOUST. L through Bullecourt	
	23.11.17	6pm	Work continued as for 22.L	

WAR DIARY
or
INTELLIGENCE SUMMARY

Army Form C. 2118.

(Erase heading not required.)

Instructions regarding War Diaries and Intelligence Summaries are contained in F. S. Regs., Part II. and the Staff Manual respectively. Title pages will be prepared in manuscript.

Place	Date	Hour	Summary of Events and Information	Remarks and references to Appendices
BEUGNATRE	24.11.17	6 pm	A, B, D Coys cleaved road from ECOUST to BULLECOURT AVENUE. 2 platoons (B Coy) loading & unloading material. C Coy cleaning road from NEW PELICAN AVE to ECOUST.	
"	25.11.17	6 pm	Work continued as for 24th. Machine gun fire from front line.	
"	26.11.17	6 pm	A, C, D Coys dug CT from old front line at U.21.c.5.1 to U.21.c.8.5. Remnis to German front line about U.21.a.10.8. Started work to about depth 3', 4', top 2' bottom. (continues) Three T. heads. B Coy cleared Mts Road to about U.20.c.5.5. Part of D Coy working on ECOUST Rd.	
"	27.11.17	6 pm	A Coy completed new CT to correct depth of 6', 5' top, 2' 6" bottom. 2 of D Coy deepening and widening SADLER LANE. Part of B Coy completed drainage from ECOUST Rd.	
"	28.11.17	6 pm	A Coy started work on NEW PELICAN AVENUE. Clearing and laying French Broad. C Coy commenced driving front line from U.21.d.H.6 - U.20×U.15 (approx). B Coy commenced work on NOREUIL - VAULX Rd.	
"	29.11.17	6 pm	Started front line from U.21.d.2.6. 120×U.15 ×35.R.D. B Coy worked on NOREUIL-VAULX Rd. A Coy continued work on NEW PELICAN AVENUE. 60× French cleared to travel breach. Laid. C+D Coys continued driving front line 240× ×35.R.D. B Coy Clearing & laying NOREUIL Rd	
"	30.11.17	6 pm	A Coy continued work on NEW PELICAN AVE. 29.M. C+D Coys continued driving 200× drive started. B Coy continued work on NOREUIL Rd. 30× Metalled road completed.	

Russell Martin
Maj. 2/1 Monm Royal Engs.

Apendix A —

This march reflects credit on the officers & men under my command the distance 84 miles was covered in 6 days — We had no stragglers — and this after having had a very hard time in the salient — I consider this was due to the following reasons —

(1) Strict march discipline was maintained throughout, halts were given at correct intervals. Haversack rations were carried, and hot tea served at midday halt. This was quicker, & found to be better than having a hot meal at mid day — & the men were able to have a good hot feed when they were in their billets —

(2) The men marched in fighting kits. Packs & blankets being carried on 4 lorries. The blankets were folded the same size as the packs & were secured by the long carrying straps, which enabled them to be packed quite easily in the lorries. Arriving at destination, they were stacked

Appendix A Cont'd

near each company's billets. Thus no time was lost in drawing them when the company arrived. Men excused medically by the Doctor were used for loading & unloading & as guards.

Roswell Martin
2nd Lt.

WAR DIARY or INTELLIGENCE SUMMARY

Army Form C. 2118.

200 R.R.R.C (Pioneers)

Vol 18

Place	Date	Hour	Summary of Events and Information	Remarks and references to Appendices
BEUGNATRE B30.c.2.2.	1.12.17	6pm	A Coy continued work on NEW PELICAN AVENUE. Registering and wiring trench brays. C Coy erected 200x wire from NEW PELICAN AVENUE. D Coy continued work front line to left - right it could be about	
	2.12.17	6pm	U.22.c.35.50. B Coy laid Hex (Jalzon) on NOREUIL-VAULX Rd Continued work on NEW PELICAN AVENUE C Coy continued 120x wire brelise	
	3.12.17	6pm	B Coy continued 60x100x plat - A Coy continued work on C.T. C Coy wired Hex pets 4x4x4/sand paradidy post. D Coy continued 120x wire - B Coy	
	4.12.17	6pm	cont 73x40x slatting in continuation of work.	
	5.12.17	6pm	A 13. D Coys continued work as pr 3/2	
	6.12.17	6pm	A Coy continued work on C.T. C & D Coys clearing JOY RIDE TRENCH & putting in duck boards. B Coy continued slatting VAULX - NOREUIL Rd	
			A Coy erected 120x 2 wire in front of JOY RIDE from SADDLER LANE - E. C Coy wired from old Lewis gun pit U.21.d.3.6	
	7.12.17	6pm	to U.21.d.1.9. D Coy wired from post U 22/6 to 76x36d line.	
			A.B.D. Coys erected 680x wire in front of PUDSEY SUPPORT from BUNNY HUG to TOWER TRENCH. C Coy wired	
	8.12.17	6pm	200x wire in front of LONDON SUPPORT working W from FOXTROT	
			A.13.D Coys continued wire in front of INKLEY SUPPORT from TOWER TRENCH to SYDNEY END. C Coy repairing	
	9.12.17	6pm	wire in front of LONDON SUPPORT between FOXTROT and BUNNY HUG	
	10.12.17	6pm	A.13. D Coys thickening wire in front of PUDSEY, INKLEY, HALIFAX SUPPORT. C Coy continued wiring LONDON SUPPORT	
	11.12.17	6pm	A.B.D Coys continued wiring from COOEE ALLEY to RAILWAY SUPPORT. C Coy continued wiring LONDON SUPPORT	
	12.12.17	6pm	All companies continued work as pr 10.12	
	13.12.17	6pm	d. 500x wire erected	
			B.C. Coys erected 420x wire in front of PONTEFRACT & DEWSBURY TRENCH. A & D Coy digging new fire trench	
	14.12.17	6pm	from RAILWAY RESERVE towards GORDON SUPPORT. 500x trench dug.	
	15.12.17	6pm	A & D Coys continued work on new fire trench. B & C Coys continued to wire up in front of 9 DEWSBURY TRENCH	
	16.12.17	6pm	The battalion moved to MORY - moves completed by 12 noon - Work continued as for 14.12	
MORY	17.12.17	6pm	Completed fire trench to N.W. end of HORSE SHOE REDOUBT, all coys working	
	18.12.17	6pm	All companies at work on wire in front of new trench 550x standard wire erected	
	19.12.17	6pm	Com pts wiring 550x wire erected	
	20.12.17	6pm	A.B.D Coy thickening wire erected 50x new joining up with 36 N Field Coy. A Coy connecting up of fire trench	
	21.12.17	6pm	and diaphragm 60x N19 Block	
	22.12.17	6pm	Battalion rested 550x wire	
			A.B.C. Coys completed 500x wire in front of TANK AVENUE. Thickening from JOY RIDE	
			and TANK AVENUE 500x wire in front of TANK AVENUE A Coy thickening wire erected on previous night	

A 5834 Wt.W4973/M687 750,000 8/16 D.D. & L. Ltd. Forms/C.2113/13.

Army Form C. 2118.

WAR DIARY
or
INTELLIGENCE SUMMARY.
(Erase heading not required.)

Instructions regarding War Diaries and Intelligence Summaries are contained in F.S. Regs., Part II. and the Staff Manual respectively. Title pages will be prepared in manuscript.

Place	Date	Hour	Summary of Events and Information	Remarks and references to Appendices
MORY	23.12.17	6 pm	All Coys. erected 750ˣ standard wire in front of TOWER SUPPORT working S.E. along unnamed trench	
"	24.12.17	6 pm	All Coys. erected 650ˣ standard wire from last night's work to A.M. line	
"	25.12.17	6 pm	B.C.D Coys. erected 650ˣ wire from bend line along MAIN AY RESERVE. A Coy. Digging from IVY RIDE to LONDON SUPPORT	
"	26.12.17		Battalion stayed last night being Christmas night.	
"	27.12.17	6 pm	Erected 550ˣ wire in front of RAILWAY RESERVE.	
"	28.12.17	6 pm	Erected 650ˣ wire in continuation of last night's work	
"	29.12.17	6 pm	Erected 550ˣ wire in continuation of last night's work in front of RAILWAY RESERVE to TIGER TRENCH	
"	30.12.17	6 pm	Moved to DURRAW Camp this Bn. resting	
"	31.12.17	6 pm	Training from 9.45.-2.30. Recreational training 2 to 4 pm	

J. Jenkins Myr
2 O/c 11th R.B.

www.ingramcontent.com/pod-product-compliance
Lightning Source LLC
Chambersburg PA
CBHW081432160426
43193CB00013B/2259